Renewable Energy Transition: Strategies for Sustainable Systems, Clean Energy Policy, and Global Solutions

Copyright

Published by Global Climate Solutions

The views expressed in this publication are those of the author and publisher, which are one and the same.

eBook ISBN: *978-1-991369-43-7*

Paperback ISBN: *978-1-991369-44-4*

Disclaimer

This publication is intended for informational purposes only. While every effort has been made to ensure the accuracy and reliability of the content, the author and publisher make no representations or warranties regarding the completeness, suitability, or applicability of the information contained herein. The content does not constitute professional, legal, investment, or energy policy advice. Readers are encouraged to consult appropriate professionals before acting on any information provided. The author and publisher shall not be held liable for any loss, damage, or disruption caused by the use or misuse of this publication.

Table of Contents

Introduction

The transition to renewable energy is one of the most critical challenges of our time. As the world faces the pressing realities of climate change, energy insecurity, and environmental degradation, the shift from fossil fuels to renewable energy systems has become a global imperative. For policymakers, this transition represents an unprecedented opportunity to not only mitigate the impacts of climate change but also foster economic growth, energy independence, and social well-being.

This chapter sets the stage for exploring the key enablers and urgent actions required to accelerate renewable energy adoption. It examines the broader context of renewable energy transitions, the vital role of policymakers, and the interconnected challenges that must be addressed. The framework introduced here provides a structured approach to navigating the complexities of renewable energy systems while ensuring sustainable and equitable outcomes. By outlining the objectives and scope of this book, this chapter serves as a roadmap for understanding the essential strategies to drive the global energy transition forward.

Importance of Renewable Energy Transition

The transition to renewable energy has emerged as one of the most pressing priorities for the 21st century. With global energy consumption continuing to rise and fossil fuel reserves dwindling, the need to shift toward sustainable energy sources is critical. Renewable energy sources, such as solar, wind, and hydropower, offer a viable alternative to fossil fuels, providing clean, abundant, and increasingly cost-effective energy. This transition is not only a necessity for combating climate change but also a vital step toward achieving long-term energy security and economic resilience.

One of the primary drivers of the renewable energy transition is the urgent need to address climate change. The continued reliance on fossil fuels has led to an alarming rise in greenhouse gas emissions, which are the primary contributors to global warming. Scientists and policymakers agree that limiting global temperature rise to 1.5°C above pre-industrial levels is essential to avoiding the most catastrophic impacts of climate change. Achieving this goal requires a dramatic reduction in carbon emissions, which can only be achieved by transitioning to renewable energy systems. Unlike fossil fuels, renewable energy sources generate electricity with minimal or no greenhouse gas emissions, making them a cornerstone of global decarbonization efforts.

Beyond environmental considerations, renewable energy offers significant economic and social benefits. Investments in renewable energy projects can stimulate job creation across multiple sectors, including manufacturing, installation, and maintenance. For example, the solar and wind energy industries are among the fastest-growing sectors globally, providing millions of jobs and supporting local economies. Additionally, the decentralized nature of renewable energy systems, such as rooftop solar panels, can enhance energy access in remote and underserved areas, empowering communities and reducing energy poverty.

Energy security is another critical advantage of transitioning to renewables. Unlike fossil fuels, which are often concentrated in specific regions and subject to geopolitical tensions, renewable energy sources are widely distributed and accessible in almost every part of the world. By diversifying energy supply through renewables, countries can reduce their dependence on imported fuels, strengthen their energy independence, and improve their resilience to external shocks such as price volatility or supply disruptions.

The cost competitiveness of renewable energy has also improved significantly in recent years, further underscoring the importance of this transition. Advances in technology, economies of scale, and supportive policies have driven down the costs of solar and wind power, making them the cheapest sources of electricity in many regions. This cost advantage not only benefits consumers but also encourages businesses and governments to prioritize renewable energy in their planning and investments.

In conclusion, the renewable energy transition is essential for addressing the interconnected challenges of climate change, energy security, and economic development. It represents an opportunity to build a more sustainable and resilient energy system that meets the needs of current and future generations. As the global energy landscape continues to evolve, the importance of renewable energy cannot be overstated. Policymakers, businesses, and individuals must work together to accelerate this transition and realize its full potential.

Role of Policymakers

Policymakers play a central role in driving the transition to renewable energy. As the stewards of regulatory frameworks, economic incentives, and public investment, they are uniquely positioned to shape the energy landscape and create the conditions necessary for sustainable energy systems to thrive. Their actions—or inaction—can significantly accelerate or hinder the adoption of renewable energy technologies, making their role pivotal in this global shift.

One of the most critical functions of policymakers is to establish clear and ambitious renewable energy targets. By setting long-term goals for renewable energy deployment, governments provide a sense of direction and certainty for stakeholders, including businesses, investors, and consumers. These targets serve as a foundation for policy development, aligning national priorities with global climate commitments, such as those outlined in the Paris Agreement. Clear targets also send a strong signal to the market, encouraging investment and innovation in renewable energy technologies.

Policymakers also design and implement regulatory frameworks that govern the development and integration of renewable energy into existing energy systems. These frameworks must address key challenges, such as grid access, energy storage, and the intermittency of renewable energy sources like wind and solar. Through regulations that ensure fair competition, grid reliability, and market transparency, policymakers can create an enabling environment that supports the growth of renewable energy while maintaining energy system stability.

Economic incentives are another powerful tool in the hands of policymakers. Subsidies, tax breaks, and feed-in tariffs can lower the financial barriers to adopting renewable energy, making it more accessible to households and businesses. At the same time, policymakers can phase out subsidies for fossil fuels, leveling the playing field for renewables and signaling a clear commitment to sustainable energy. Innovative financing mechanisms, such as green bonds or public-private partnerships, can further mobilize resources for renewable energy projects.

Public investment in research, development, and infrastructure is another area where policymakers play a crucial role. Funding research and innovation can drive technological advancements, reducing the costs and increasing the efficiency of renewable energy systems. Additionally, investing in critical infrastructure, such as smart grids and energy storage solutions, ensures that renewable energy can be effectively integrated and distributed.

Policymakers must also engage in international collaboration to address the global nature of the renewable energy transition. By participating in multilateral agreements, sharing best practices, and fostering cross-border partnerships, they can help harmonize standards and facilitate technology transfer. This is particularly important for developing countries, where access to technical and financial resources may be limited.

Finally, policymakers have a responsibility to ensure that the renewable energy transition is inclusive and equitable. This includes addressing energy poverty, supporting vulnerable communities, and creating opportunities for workforce development in renewable energy sectors. Policymakers must consider the social and economic impacts of their decisions, ensuring that no one is left behind in the shift to a sustainable energy future.

Framework of Enablers and Actions

The renewable energy transition requires a comprehensive framework of enablers and actions to address the challenges and harness the opportunities associated with this shift. These enablers act as foundational pillars that support the adoption and scaling of renewable energy technologies, while the actions define the specific measures required to implement these enablers effectively. Together, they form a roadmap for policymakers to guide the transition toward a sustainable energy future.

Policy and Regulation

Policy and regulation form the backbone of the renewable energy transition framework. Policymakers must establish clear, long-term objectives that set the direction for renewable energy development. These objectives should align with global climate goals and be complemented by national targets that consider local resources and capacities. Policies should incentivize the adoption of renewables through mechanisms such as tax credits, subsidies, and renewable portfolio standards. At the same time, regulatory frameworks must be adaptive to evolving technologies and market conditions, ensuring fair competition, grid reliability, and environmental protection.

Key actions in this area include:

1. Setting ambitious but realistic renewable energy targets.

2. Creating transparent permitting processes to reduce delays in project development.

3. Phasing out subsidies for fossil fuels to create a level playing field for renewables.

Supply Chains, Skills, and Capacities

The transition to renewable energy requires robust supply chains, skilled labor, and institutional capacities. Supply chains must be resilient, local, and capable of delivering the components necessary for renewable energy systems. Simultaneously, a skilled workforce is critical to design, install, and maintain these systems. Policymakers must foster partnerships with educational institutions and industry to create training programs tailored to renewable energy technologies.

Key actions in this area include:

1. Investing in workforce development initiatives to address skill gaps.

2. Localizing supply chains to reduce reliance on imports and enhance energy security.

3. Building institutional capacities to manage renewable energy systems effectively.

Finance

Financing is a critical enabler of the renewable energy transition. Policymakers must mobilize financial resources through public and private investment. Scaling up financing for renewable energy projects requires innovative mechanisms such as green bonds, public-private partnerships, and concessional loans. Equally important is the equitable distribution of financing, ensuring that developing countries and underserved communities have access to the resources needed to adopt renewable energy.

Key actions in this area include:

1. Establishing financial incentives to reduce the cost of renewable energy technologies.

2. Encouraging private-sector investment through risk-sharing mechanisms.

3. Allocating public funds to support research, development, and demonstration projects.

International Collaboration

Given the global nature of energy markets and climate challenges, international collaboration is essential. Policymakers must participate in multilateral agreements and foster partnerships that facilitate the exchange of knowledge, technologies, and resources. Collaborative efforts can help harmonize standards, reduce costs, and ensure equitable access to renewable energy solutions.

Key actions in this area include:

1. Joining international initiatives focused on renewable energy development.

2. Sharing best practices and lessons learned across borders.

3. Facilitating technology transfer to developing nations to promote equity.

Infrastructure and System Operation

Modernizing energy infrastructure is a prerequisite for integrating renewable energy into existing systems. This includes upgrading transmission and distribution networks, implementing smart grid technologies, and investing in energy storage solutions. Policymakers must ensure that infrastructure development is aligned with renewable energy goals, creating systems that are both efficient and resilient.

Key actions in this area include:

1. Upgrading grid infrastructure to accommodate intermittent renewable energy sources.

2. Deploying energy storage systems to ensure grid stability and reliability.

3. Promoting decentralized energy systems, such as rooftop solar and microgrids, to enhance resilience.

Integration of Cross-Cutting Issues

The renewable energy transition cannot be addressed in isolation from other pressing issues, such as social equity, economic development, and environmental conservation. Policymakers must adopt a holistic approach that considers these cross-cutting issues. For example, ensuring equitable access to renewable energy is vital for reducing energy poverty, while incorporating circular economy principles can minimize waste and maximize resource efficiency.

Key actions in this area include:

1. Designing policies that prioritize energy access for underserved communities.

2. Promoting sustainable manufacturing and recycling practices for renewable energy components.

3. Addressing the social and economic impacts of the transition, such as job displacement in fossil fuel industries.

Monitoring and Evaluation

A robust framework must also include mechanisms for monitoring and evaluation. Policymakers need reliable data to assess the effectiveness of their actions and make informed decisions. Establishing transparent monitoring systems ensures accountability and provides opportunities for course correction.

Key actions in this area include:

1. Developing key performance indicators (KPIs) to track progress toward renewable energy goals.

2. Establishing independent bodies to evaluate policy effectiveness.

3. Using data-driven insights to refine and improve policies over time.

Linking Enablers and Actions

The enablers described above are deeply interconnected, and their success depends on coordinated actions across multiple domains. For example, scaling up financing requires robust regulatory frameworks and international collaboration to attract investment. Similarly, developing supply chains and infrastructure relies on workforce development and public funding. Policymakers must adopt an integrated approach, recognizing the synergies between these enablers and designing actions that maximize their collective impact.

In conclusion, this framework provides policymakers with a comprehensive roadmap for driving the renewable energy transition. By focusing on these key enablers—policy and regulation, supply chains and skills, finance, international collaboration, infrastructure, and cross-cutting issues—policymakers can create the conditions necessary for a sustainable energy future. The specific actions outlined in this framework serve as practical steps to address challenges, seize opportunities, and accelerate progress.

Objectives and Structure of the Book

The primary objective of this book is to provide policymakers with a comprehensive guide to accelerating the renewable energy transition. By focusing on actionable strategies, this book aims to empower decision-makers to address the challenges of energy decarbonization while ensuring economic growth, energy security, and environmental sustainability. As renewable energy becomes a central pillar of climate action and economic development, the book emphasizes the urgent need for clear policies, robust infrastructure, and inclusive international collaboration.

A key goal of this book is to present a structured framework of enablers and actions that can guide policymakers in designing and implementing effective renewable energy strategies. This framework is built on five foundational enablers: policy and regulation, supply chains and capacities, finance, international collaboration, and infrastructure and system operation. Each enabler is explored in depth, offering readers insights into its role, challenges, and opportunities within the broader energy transition landscape.

This book also aims to highlight the interconnected nature of these enablers. While each chapter provides a detailed examination of specific themes, the book consistently emphasizes the importance of integration. Policymakers are encouraged to view these enablers not as isolated pillars but as components of a cohesive strategy that requires coordination across sectors and regions.

Another key objective is to provide a forward-looking perspective on renewable energy transitions. The book explores not only current challenges but also the evolving opportunities presented by technological innovation, global partnerships, and shifting economic priorities. By offering a future-focused lens, this book equips policymakers to anticipate and adapt to emerging trends, ensuring their strategies remain relevant and impactful in the years to come.

The structure of the book reflects these objectives. It begins with an introduction that outlines the importance of renewable energy, the critical role of policymakers, and the framework of enablers and actions that underpins the book. The following five sections are dedicated to each of the enablers. These sections delve into specific challenges, opportunities, and actionable solutions, with a neutral tone that provides practical guidance without relying on case studies.

The book's final chapter ties together the key insights and strategies from the previous sections, offering policymakers a clear summary of the actions required to achieve a successful renewable energy transition. It concludes with recommendations for future efforts, emphasizing the importance of collaboration, innovation, and adaptability in navigating the complexities of the energy landscape.

In summary, the objectives of this book are to equip policymakers with a clear understanding of the enablers of renewable energy transitions, provide actionable guidance, and foster a holistic approach to energy policy design and implementation. Through its structured framework and forward-looking perspective, this book serves as a practical resource for policymakers working to build a sustainable and equitable energy future.

Chapter 1: Adapting Policies for a Renewable Future

The transition to renewable energy requires a transformative shift in policy frameworks to enable the widespread adoption of clean and sustainable energy systems. Policymakers play a pivotal role in creating the regulatory and economic environment necessary to drive this transition. Without clear, forward-thinking policies, the full potential of renewable energy technologies may remain unrealized, and global climate goals could fall out of reach.

This chapter explores how adaptive policies can serve as a catalyst for renewable energy deployment. It examines the foundational elements of effective energy policies, including setting ambitious yet achievable targets, designing financial incentives, and aligning national priorities with international commitments. The chapter also addresses the importance of regulatory flexibility to accommodate evolving technologies and market conditions, ensuring that policies remain relevant and effective over time.

By providing a detailed overview of key policy instruments and their implementation, this chapter offers policymakers a roadmap to design frameworks that not only accelerate renewable energy transitions but also promote economic growth, energy security, and social equity. The insights presented here lay the foundation for understanding how well-crafted policies can lead to a sustainable and resilient energy future.

Importance of Renewable Energy Policies

Renewable energy policies are vital for enabling the transition from fossil fuel-based systems to sustainable and clean energy solutions. These policies set the foundation for advancing renewable energy adoption, addressing climate change, and meeting growing energy demands while ensuring economic development and social equity. Without clear and robust policies, the renewable energy sector cannot achieve its full potential or contribute effectively to global energy transformation.

One of the primary reasons renewable energy policies are important is their role in reducing greenhouse gas emissions. Fossil fuel-based energy production is the largest contributor to global carbon dioxide emissions, driving climate change and its associated impacts, such as extreme weather events, rising sea levels, and biodiversity loss. Renewable energy, by contrast, provides a low-emission alternative, offering solutions to decarbonize power generation, heating, cooling, and transportation. Policies create the framework necessary for accelerating this shift, ensuring that renewable energy sources replace carbon-intensive systems at the scale and speed required to meet climate goals, such as those outlined in the Paris Agreement.

Policies also provide the necessary signals to investors and businesses. Clear renewable energy targets and supportive policies reduce uncertainty and encourage investment in renewable energy infrastructure, technologies, and innovation. They foster a stable and predictable environment where private sector stakeholders are more willing to allocate resources to long-term renewable energy projects. Without these signals, the financial risks associated with renewable energy investments may outweigh the potential benefits, slowing the pace of deployment.

Economic growth and job creation are other significant benefits driven by renewable energy policies. The renewable energy sector has become a major source of employment globally, with millions of jobs created in areas such as solar panel manufacturing, wind turbine installation, and system maintenance. Policymakers play a critical role in sustaining this growth by implementing incentives, subsidies, and other mechanisms that lower barriers to market entry and stimulate industry expansion. Policies that support training and workforce development further ensure that economies have the skills needed to meet the growing demand for renewable energy expertise.

Another essential role of renewable energy policies is to enhance energy security. Fossil fuels are finite resources that are often concentrated in specific geographic regions, making countries dependent on imports and vulnerable to supply disruptions or price volatility. Renewable energy, on the other hand, is derived from abundant, locally available resources such as sunlight, wind, and water. By creating policies that prioritize the development and integration of renewables, governments can reduce reliance on foreign energy sources and enhance national energy independence.

Social equity is also a critical dimension addressed by renewable energy policies. Access to affordable and reliable energy is fundamental to improving quality of life and reducing poverty. However, traditional energy systems often fail to reach remote or underserved areas. Policies that promote decentralized renewable energy systems, such as rooftop solar or community microgrids, can help bridge this gap, bringing clean energy to regions that have historically been marginalized. This ensures that the benefits of the renewable energy transition are distributed equitably, fostering greater social inclusion.

In addition to addressing environmental and socio-economic challenges, renewable energy policies drive technological innovation. By supporting research and development, governments can spur advancements in efficiency, storage, and grid integration, making renewable energy systems more competitive and versatile. Policies that incentivize innovation also help to lower costs, enabling renewables to compete with traditional energy sources in terms of affordability.

Furthermore, renewable energy policies are essential for integrating renewables into existing energy systems. Transitioning to renewable energy requires addressing technical challenges such as intermittency, grid stability, and energy storage. Policies play a pivotal role in modernizing energy infrastructure, such as implementing smart grids and expanding storage capacity, to accommodate the unique characteristics of renewable energy sources.

Finally, renewable energy policies provide a framework for aligning national priorities with global commitments. Climate change and energy transformation are global challenges that require coordinated international efforts. Policies help countries fulfill their obligations under agreements like the Paris Agreement, enabling them to contribute to collective goals while addressing domestic energy needs.

Key Policy Instruments: Targets, Mandates, and Incentives

The adoption of renewable energy requires a structured set of policy instruments to guide and accelerate the transition. Among the most effective tools at the disposal of policymakers are targets, mandates, and incentives. Each of these instruments plays a unique role in driving the deployment of renewable energy technologies, fostering market growth, and ensuring alignment with national and global sustainability goals. By implementing a combination of these approaches, policymakers can create an enabling environment that supports renewable energy adoption while addressing economic, social, and environmental objectives.

Targets: Setting a Clear Vision for Renewable Energy

Renewable energy targets provide a roadmap for energy transition, offering clear and measurable goals for governments, industries, and stakeholders. Targets are often expressed as a percentage of total energy consumption or generation to be sourced from renewables by a specific year. These goals serve as benchmarks that align national efforts with global commitments such as the Paris Agreement and the United Nations Sustainable Development Goals.

Targets help reduce market uncertainty by providing a long-term vision for the energy sector. They signal a government's commitment to renewable energy, which encourages investment and innovation. For example, countries that establish ambitious renewable energy targets often attract private-sector investment and international funding, boosting the deployment of renewable energy projects. Targets also serve as a foundation for other policy instruments, such as mandates and incentives, ensuring consistency in policy frameworks.

To be effective, renewable energy targets must be ambitious yet achievable, reflecting the country's available resources, technological capacity, and socio-economic context. They should also include interim milestones to track progress and enable course corrections when needed. For example, a target might specify achieving 50% renewable electricity generation by 2030, with incremental goals of 20% by 2025 and 35% by 2027.

Mandates: Enforcing Renewable Energy Adoption

Mandates are regulatory requirements that compel specific entities, such as utilities or industries, to adopt renewable energy or achieve certain sustainability standards. Unlike targets, which provide voluntary direction, mandates are enforceable and typically accompanied by penalties for non-compliance. Mandates are essential for ensuring that renewable energy adoption is not left to market forces alone but is actively driven by government intervention.

One common form of mandate is the Renewable Portfolio Standard (RPS), which requires electricity providers to ensure that a specified percentage of their energy supply comes from renewable sources. For example, an RPS might mandate that utilities generate 25% of their electricity from wind, solar, or other renewables by a given date. This approach has been widely adopted in both developed and developing countries, helping to create demand for renewable energy and stimulate market growth.

Another example of a mandate is the use of building codes and standards to promote renewable energy integration in construction. Governments may require new buildings to install solar panels, incorporate energy-efficient designs, or use renewable energy for heating and cooling systems. Similarly, transportation mandates, such as biofuel blending requirements, encourage the adoption of renewable energy in the transport sector.

Mandates also play a critical role in addressing barriers to renewable energy adoption, such as grid access and reliability. For instance, policies may require grid operators to prioritize renewable energy over fossil fuel generation, ensuring that renewables have guaranteed access to electricity markets.

Incentives: Reducing Financial Barriers

Incentives are among the most powerful tools for promoting renewable energy adoption, as they directly address the financial challenges associated with deploying new technologies. These instruments reduce the upfront costs of renewable energy systems, making them more accessible to households, businesses, and industries. By lowering financial barriers, incentives encourage widespread adoption and accelerate the transition to a sustainable energy system.

One of the most common forms of incentive is the feed-in tariff (FiT), which guarantees renewable energy producers a fixed price for the electricity they generate over a specified period. FiTs provide financial certainty for investors and help ensure that renewable energy projects are economically viable. They have been particularly successful in countries like Germany, where FiTs played a key role in driving the rapid deployment of solar and wind energy.

Tax incentives are another widely used policy instrument. These include tax credits, deductions, and exemptions that reduce the overall cost of renewable energy projects. For example, investment tax credits (ITCs) allow businesses and individuals to deduct a percentage of the cost of installing renewable energy systems, such as solar panels or wind turbines. Production tax credits (PTCs), on the other hand, provide financial rewards based on the amount of renewable energy generated.

Governments also offer grants and subsidies to support renewable energy deployment. These funds can be used for research and development, pilot projects, or large-scale installations. Subsidies for renewable energy equipment, such as solar panels and batteries, further lower costs and encourage adoption at the household level. In some cases, governments provide low-interest loans or loan guarantees to finance renewable energy projects, making them more attractive to private investors.

Net metering is another incentive that encourages renewable energy adoption by allowing consumers to sell excess electricity generated by their systems, such as rooftop solar panels, back to the grid. This not only reduces electricity bills but also provides an additional income stream, making renewable energy systems more financially appealing.

Integration of Policy Instruments

While each policy instrument—targets, mandates, and incentives— serves a distinct purpose, their effectiveness is maximized when used in combination. For instance, clear renewable energy targets can provide the overarching vision, while mandates enforce compliance, and incentives reduce the financial burden of adoption. This integrated approach ensures that policies are mutually reinforcing and aligned with broader sustainability goals.

For example, a country might set a target of 50% renewable energy generation by 2030, supported by an RPS that requires utilities to procure a minimum percentage of their electricity from renewables. At the same time, tax incentives and feed-in tariffs could encourage private investment in renewable energy projects, while subsidies make renewable energy systems affordable for households and small businesses.

Challenges and Considerations

While these policy instruments are effective, their implementation requires careful consideration to ensure equity, efficiency, and sustainability. Policymakers must address potential drawbacks, such as the risk of over-subsidization, market distortions, or inequitable distribution of benefits. Additionally, policies should be regularly reviewed and updated to reflect changes in technology, market conditions, and societal needs.

Policy Implementation Frameworks

The success of renewable energy policies depends not only on their design but also on their effective implementation. A robust policy implementation framework ensures that the objectives of renewable energy policies are translated into tangible outcomes. This involves aligning regulatory processes, institutional capacities, stakeholder engagement, and monitoring mechanisms to facilitate the smooth adoption and integration of renewable energy systems. Policymakers must create frameworks that are adaptable, inclusive, and capable of addressing both technical and socio-economic challenges.

A critical component of policy implementation is the establishment of clear regulatory processes. These processes should provide guidelines for project development, permitting, and compliance while minimizing bureaucratic hurdles. Streamlined permitting procedures are essential to avoid delays in renewable energy projects. For example, simplified approval processes for installing solar panels or wind farms can significantly accelerate project timelines. Transparent regulatory frameworks also help build trust among investors, developers, and communities, encouraging broader participation in renewable energy initiatives.

Institutional capacity is another vital element of effective policy implementation. Governments and agencies tasked with implementing renewable energy policies must have the resources, expertise, and infrastructure required to manage complex energy systems. This includes training personnel, modernizing energy infrastructure, and ensuring that regulatory bodies have the technical knowledge to oversee renewable energy integration. Collaboration between government institutions and private entities can further enhance capacity and facilitate knowledge transfer.

Stakeholder engagement is equally important in the implementation of renewable energy policies. Policymakers must involve diverse stakeholders, including local communities, industry players, and non-governmental organizations, in the planning and execution of renewable energy projects. Early engagement helps identify potential challenges, build consensus, and address community concerns. It also fosters a sense of ownership among stakeholders, increasing the likelihood of project success. For example, involving local communities in decision-making can mitigate opposition to renewable energy projects, such as wind farms, by addressing concerns about visual impacts or land use.

Monitoring and evaluation mechanisms are essential for assessing the effectiveness of policy implementation frameworks. Policymakers need reliable data to track progress toward renewable energy targets and identify areas for improvement. Establishing performance indicators, such as the percentage of energy generated from renewables or reductions in greenhouse gas emissions, enables governments to measure the impact of their policies. Regular reporting and independent audits ensure accountability and provide opportunities for course correction.

Adaptability is another key feature of successful policy implementation frameworks. Renewable energy technologies and markets are constantly evolving, requiring policies to be flexible and responsive to change. Policymakers must periodically review and update their frameworks to reflect advancements in technology, shifts in market dynamics, and emerging societal needs. For instance, as energy storage technologies become more affordable, policies may need to prioritize their integration into existing systems.

Chapter 2: Regulatory Mechanisms for Energy Transition

Regulatory mechanisms are the cornerstone of a successful energy transition, providing the rules, guidelines, and structures necessary to integrate renewable energy into existing systems. As renewable energy technologies continue to evolve and expand, regulators face the challenge of balancing the needs of innovation, market growth, and grid reliability. Effective regulatory mechanisms not only facilitate the adoption of renewables but also ensure a fair, transparent, and competitive energy market.

This chapter explores the critical role of regulatory frameworks in driving the energy transition. It delves into the challenges of integrating renewable energy sources, such as intermittency and grid compatibility, and examines how well-designed regulations can address these issues. From market reforms and grid access rules to energy pricing models, this chapter provides insights into the regulatory strategies that can create a supportive environment for renewable energy.

By focusing on practical solutions and emerging trends, this chapter aims to equip policymakers and stakeholders with the tools to design and implement effective regulatory mechanisms. These mechanisms are essential for ensuring that the transition to renewable energy is not only technically viable but also economically sustainable and socially inclusive.

Challenges of Integrating Renewables

The integration of renewable energy into existing energy systems presents a range of challenges that policymakers and energy stakeholders must address to ensure a smooth transition. Renewable energy sources such as solar, wind, and hydropower offer significant environmental and economic benefits, but their unique characteristics can strain traditional energy systems. From issues related to intermittency to the need for infrastructure upgrades, these challenges require innovative solutions and coordinated efforts to overcome.

Intermittency and Variability

One of the most prominent challenges of integrating renewables is their intermittent and variable nature. Unlike fossil fuels, which can provide a consistent and controllable energy supply, renewable energy sources like solar and wind are dependent on weather conditions. Solar panels generate electricity only during daylight hours, and wind turbines require sufficient wind speeds to operate efficiently. This variability creates difficulties in matching energy supply with demand, particularly during peak usage periods.

To address this challenge, energy systems must become more flexible and adaptable. Solutions include the deployment of energy storage technologies, such as batteries, to store excess energy generated during periods of high production for use during low-production times. Additionally, demand response programs, which incentivize consumers to adjust their energy usage during peak periods, can help balance supply and demand.

Grid Stability and Reliability

The integration of large-scale renewable energy sources can pose risks to grid stability and reliability. Traditional grids were designed to accommodate centralized power generation from fossil fuel plants, which provide a steady flow of electricity. In contrast, renewables are often distributed and decentralized, feeding energy into the grid from multiple sources at varying levels. This can create fluctuations in voltage and frequency, potentially destabilizing the grid.

Grid operators need to adopt advanced technologies and practices to maintain stability. Smart grid systems, which use digital communication technologies to monitor and manage energy flows in real time, can help balance the grid and ensure reliable power delivery. Investments in grid modernization, including upgraded transmission and distribution networks, are also critical for accommodating the decentralized nature of renewable energy.

Infrastructure Limitations

Existing energy infrastructure is often ill-equipped to support the integration of renewables. Transmission and distribution networks, in particular, may lack the capacity to handle the increased load and variability associated with renewable energy generation. For instance, wind farms are frequently located in remote areas far from population centers, requiring extensive transmission lines to deliver electricity to consumers. Similarly, rooftop solar installations can create reverse energy flows that existing infrastructure may not be designed to manage.

Expanding and upgrading energy infrastructure is essential to overcome these limitations. Policymakers must prioritize investments in new transmission lines, substations, and energy storage facilities. Additionally, integrating decentralized energy systems, such as microgrids, can enhance local energy resilience and reduce the strain on centralized infrastructure.

Market and Regulatory Barriers

The transition to renewable energy is often hindered by market and regulatory barriers that favor fossil fuels or fail to account for the unique characteristics of renewables. For example, legacy energy markets may prioritize large-scale, continuous power generation, making it difficult for renewable energy producers to compete. Regulatory frameworks may also impose burdensome permitting processes or fail to incentivize renewable energy adoption.

Reforming energy markets and regulatory frameworks is crucial to creating a level playing field for renewables. Policies such as feed-in tariffs, renewable portfolio standards, and carbon pricing can provide the financial and regulatory support needed to drive renewable energy growth. Simplifying permitting processes and reducing bureaucratic hurdles can also accelerate the development of renewable energy projects.

Public Acceptance and Land Use

Public acceptance and land use conflicts can pose significant challenges to renewable energy integration. Large-scale renewable energy projects, such as wind farms or solar arrays, often require significant land area and can face opposition from local communities. Concerns about visual impacts, noise, and environmental disruption can delay or halt project development.

Engaging with local communities early in the planning process and addressing their concerns can help build public support for renewable energy projects. Offering community benefits, such as job creation or revenue-sharing agreements, can further enhance acceptance. Additionally, adopting best practices for site selection, such as prioritizing degraded or underutilized land, can minimize environmental and social impacts.

Energy Storage and Technological Gaps

The lack of affordable and efficient energy storage solutions is a significant barrier to renewable energy integration. While technologies such as lithium-ion batteries have advanced in recent years, they remain expensive and face limitations in terms of capacity and lifespan. Developing alternative storage technologies, such as pumped hydro, thermal storage, or hydrogen, is essential for overcoming this challenge.

Policymakers and researchers must prioritize funding for energy storage innovation and deployment. Expanding research and development efforts, incentivizing private sector investment, and supporting pilot projects can accelerate the commercialization of advanced storage technologies.

Regulatory Reforms and Market Design

The transition to renewable energy requires comprehensive regulatory reforms and innovative market designs to overcome systemic barriers and facilitate the large-scale integration of renewable energy sources. Traditional energy markets were built around centralized fossil fuel-based power generation, which poses significant challenges to the adoption of decentralized, variable renewable energy systems. Policymakers must redesign regulatory frameworks and market structures to create a supportive environment for renewable energy, ensuring reliability, fairness, and cost-effectiveness.

The Need for Regulatory Reforms

Regulatory reforms are essential to address outdated policies and align them with the unique requirements of renewable energy. Traditional regulatory frameworks often favor fossil fuel generation due to historical infrastructure investments, subsidies, and operational practices. These systems typically prioritize baseload power plants, which generate consistent energy, while renewables like solar and wind are variable and distributed. Reforms are necessary to ensure renewable energy is integrated effectively without compromising grid stability or market competitiveness.

Key areas for regulatory reform include grid access, pricing mechanisms, permitting processes, and emissions regulations. By removing barriers and creating incentives, regulatory reforms can encourage investment in renewable energy and support its integration into energy markets.

Grid Access and Interconnection Reforms

One of the most critical areas of regulatory reform involves ensuring equitable grid access for renewable energy producers. Historically, centralized fossil fuel plants have enjoyed guaranteed grid access, while renewable energy systems often face technical and regulatory barriers. For example, small-scale renewable energy producers, such as rooftop solar installations, may encounter challenges connecting to the grid due to complex interconnection standards or high fees.

Reforms should streamline interconnection processes, reduce fees for renewable energy producers, and prioritize grid upgrades to accommodate distributed generation. Additionally, grid operators should implement transparent rules that guarantee renewable energy producers access to the grid while maintaining system reliability. Priority dispatch for renewable energy, where grid operators are required to integrate renewables before fossil fuel generation, is another effective reform to support renewable energy adoption.

Dynamic Pricing Mechanisms

Traditional energy markets often rely on fixed pricing mechanisms that fail to reflect the variable nature of renewable energy generation. Dynamic pricing models, such as time-of-use (TOU) tariffs, can better align electricity costs with real-time supply and demand, incentivizing the efficient use of renewable energy. Under TOU tariffs, electricity prices are higher during peak demand periods and lower when renewable energy supply is abundant, encouraging consumers to shift their energy usage accordingly.

Another innovative pricing mechanism is real-time pricing, where electricity prices fluctuate based on market conditions and renewable energy availability. Real-time pricing enables consumers and businesses to make informed decisions about their energy use, optimizing consumption patterns and reducing strain on the grid.

Policymakers can also introduce mechanisms like feed-in tariffs (FiTs) and PPAs to guarantee stable revenue for renewable energy producers. FiTs offer long-term contracts with fixed rates for electricity generated from renewables, providing financial certainty for investors. PPAs allow producers to sell electricity directly to consumers or utilities under pre-negotiated terms, fostering market participation and competition.

Permitting and Licensing Reforms

Lengthy permitting and licensing processes are significant barriers to renewable energy development. Complex regulations and bureaucratic delays can deter investment, increase project costs, and slow deployment. Regulatory reforms should focus on simplifying and accelerating these processes to facilitate renewable energy growth.

One approach is to establish standardized permitting procedures for renewable energy projects, reducing administrative burdens and ensuring consistency across regions. Policymakers can also create "one-stop-shop" systems, where developers can complete all necessary permitting steps through a single platform or agency. These streamlined processes save time and resources for both developers and regulators.

In addition, governments should set clear timelines for permit approvals and establish mechanisms for resolving disputes efficiently. Transparent and predictable permitting frameworks encourage investor confidence and promote renewable energy deployment.

Market Design for Renewable Energy Integration

Effective market design is critical for integrating renewable energy into energy systems. Traditional energy markets prioritize baseload generation, which can disadvantage renewable energy producers due to their variable output. Policymakers must redesign market structures to accommodate the characteristics of renewable energy while ensuring reliability and affordability.

One key element of market design is the creation of capacity markets, where energy producers are compensated not only for the electricity they generate but also for their ability to provide capacity when needed. Capacity markets incentivize investments in energy storage, demand response, and flexible generation, which are essential for balancing renewable energy supply and demand.

Another important market mechanism is the implementation of ancillary service markets. These markets compensate energy producers for providing grid-stabilizing services, such as frequency regulation and voltage control. Renewable energy producers with advanced technologies, such as smart inverters, can participate in these markets, contributing to grid reliability and earning additional revenue.

Carbon Pricing and Emissions Trading

Carbon pricing is a powerful regulatory tool for promoting renewable energy and reducing greenhouse gas emissions. By assigning a monetary value to carbon emissions, carbon pricing mechanisms create financial incentives for businesses and utilities to adopt cleaner energy sources. Policymakers can implement carbon pricing through two primary approaches: carbon taxes and cap-and-trade systems.

Carbon taxes impose a fixed fee on carbon emissions, encouraging emitters to reduce their carbon footprint or switch to renewable energy. Cap-and-trade systems, also known as emissions trading schemes, establish a market for carbon allowances, where companies can buy or sell permits to emit a certain amount of carbon. These systems create a financial advantage for renewable energy producers, as their operations are typically carbon-free.

Revenue generated from carbon pricing can be reinvested in renewable energy projects, grid upgrades, and energy efficiency initiatives, further accelerating the energy transition.

International Coordination and Harmonization

Renewable energy markets are increasingly interconnected, requiring international coordination to ensure efficient integration and trade. Policymakers should collaborate across borders to harmonize regulations, establish common standards, and facilitate cross-border energy trading. For example, interconnected energy markets, such as the European Union's Internal Energy Market, enable countries to share renewable energy resources, optimize grid operations, and enhance energy security.

Harmonized regulations also reduce barriers for renewable energy developers operating in multiple jurisdictions, encouraging investment and innovation. By fostering international cooperation, policymakers can create a more integrated and resilient global energy market.

Challenges and Considerations

While regulatory reforms and market design offer significant benefits, they also present challenges that must be carefully managed. Policymakers must balance the interests of various stakeholders, including utilities, renewable energy developers, and consumers, to ensure fair and equitable outcomes. Additionally, reforms must account for regional differences in energy systems, resource availability, and economic conditions.

Another consideration is the potential for unintended consequences, such as market distortions or increased costs for consumers. Policymakers should implement reforms gradually, monitor their impact, and adjust policies as needed to address emerging issues.

Aligning Regulations with Goals

Aligning energy regulations with renewable energy goals is a critical step in ensuring the success of the global energy transition. Regulatory frameworks must be carefully designed to support the achievement of national and international targets, such as those set out in the Paris Agreement or specific renewable energy deployment objectives. This alignment ensures that policies are cohesive, effective, and adaptable to the evolving needs of energy systems and markets.

The first step in aligning regulations with goals is to establish clear and measurable objectives. Policymakers need to define specific targets for renewable energy adoption, such as the percentage of electricity generation from renewable sources by a certain year. These targets should consider a country's resource availability, technological capabilities, and socio-economic context. Once targets are set, regulatory frameworks must be tailored to create an enabling environment for achieving these objectives.

One critical aspect of alignment is the creation of supportive grid access rules. Renewable energy producers often face challenges in connecting to the grid, particularly in systems designed for centralized fossil fuel generation. Regulations should prioritize renewable energy integration by streamlining interconnection processes, reducing fees, and ensuring transparent and equitable grid access. For example, policies such as priority dispatch can mandate that electricity from renewable sources is integrated into the grid before fossil fuel-based generation.

Economic incentives also play a vital role in aligning regulations with renewable energy goals. FiTs, tax incentives, and renewable energy credits are examples of regulatory mechanisms that encourage investment in renewables. These incentives reduce financial barriers, making renewable energy projects more viable for developers and investors. Additionally, regulations should phase out subsidies for fossil fuels, leveling the playing field and signaling a strong commitment to clean energy.

Another important area is the alignment of emissions standards and carbon pricing mechanisms with renewable energy targets. Regulations that impose strict emissions limits on power plants and other energy-intensive industries can drive the transition to cleaner energy sources. Carbon pricing, whether through taxes or cap-and-trade systems, further incentivizes the shift to renewables by making fossil fuel generation more expensive.

Flexibility and adaptability are key to maintaining alignment between regulations and goals. Renewable energy technologies and markets evolve rapidly, requiring regulatory frameworks to be periodically reviewed and updated. Policymakers should incorporate mechanisms for monitoring and evaluation, ensuring that regulations remain relevant and effective in achieving renewable energy targets. For example, data-driven assessments of grid performance and market dynamics can inform necessary adjustments to policies.

Finally, public and stakeholder engagement is crucial for aligning regulations with broader energy goals. By involving communities, businesses, and energy producers in the regulatory process, policymakers can ensure that regulations address diverse needs and build widespread support for renewable energy initiatives.

Chapter 3: Developing Resilient Supply Chains

The rapid expansion of renewable energy systems depends on the development of resilient and efficient supply chains. Renewable energy technologies, such as solar panels, wind turbines, and energy storage systems, require extensive networks for the sourcing, production, and distribution of components. However, supply chains for renewable energy often face challenges, including resource constraints, geopolitical risks, and disruptions from global events such as pandemics or trade conflicts.

This chapter explores the critical role of supply chains in enabling the renewable energy transition and examines strategies for building resilience in these systems. It discusses the importance of localizing supply chains to enhance energy security, reducing dependence on imports, and fostering economic growth. Additionally, the chapter highlights the need for sustainable and ethical practices in the sourcing and production of renewable energy materials.

By addressing key vulnerabilities and proposing actionable solutions, this chapter provides a roadmap for policymakers, businesses, and stakeholders to strengthen supply chains and ensure the reliable delivery of renewable energy technologies. Developing resilient supply chains is not only essential for meeting renewable energy targets but also for creating a more sustainable and equitable global energy landscape.

Importance of Renewable Energy Supply Chains

Renewable energy supply chains play a critical role in facilitating the transition from fossil fuels to sustainable energy systems. These supply chains encompass the sourcing, manufacturing, transportation, and distribution of the components necessary for renewable energy technologies, such as solar panels, wind turbines, and batteries. The reliability, efficiency, and resilience of these supply chains directly impact the pace and scale of renewable energy deployment. As the global demand for clean energy grows, strengthening renewable energy supply chains has become a top priority for policymakers, businesses, and stakeholders.

Enabling the Renewable Energy Transition

Renewable energy supply chains are essential for ensuring the availability of key materials and technologies required for renewable energy systems. For example, solar panels rely on rare earth elements, such as silicon and cadmium, while wind turbines require critical metals like neodymium and copper. Batteries, which are crucial for energy storage, depend on materials such as lithium, cobalt, and nickel. A well-functioning supply chain ensures that these resources are efficiently sourced, processed, and delivered to manufacturers and end-users, enabling the deployment of renewable energy projects.

The transition to renewable energy requires a significant scaling up of production and distribution capacities. For instance, achieving global climate goals such as net-zero emissions by 2050 will necessitate the deployment of millions of solar panels and wind turbines, as well as large-scale energy storage systems. Supply chains must be capable of meeting these demands while minimizing delays and cost overruns. Without robust supply chains, the renewable energy transition could stall, jeopardizing efforts to combat climate change and reduce greenhouse gas emissions.

Enhancing Energy Security

Strong renewable energy supply chains contribute to energy security by reducing reliance on imported fossil fuels and centralized energy systems. Unlike fossil fuels, which are often concentrated in specific regions and subject to geopolitical risks, renewable energy resources such as sunlight and wind are widely distributed. By developing localized supply chains for renewable energy technologies, countries can enhance their energy independence and resilience to external disruptions.

Localization of supply chains also reduces exposure to global trade conflicts, natural disasters, and pandemics, which can disrupt the flow of critical materials. For example, the COVID-19 pandemic highlighted vulnerabilities in global supply chains, causing delays in the production and deployment of renewable energy technologies. Strengthening domestic and regional supply chains can mitigate these risks and ensure a steady supply of renewable energy components.

Supporting Economic Growth and Job Creation

Renewable energy supply chains contribute significantly to economic growth and job creation. From raw material extraction and manufacturing to installation and maintenance, supply chains generate employment opportunities across multiple sectors. For example, the expansion of the solar and wind energy industries has created millions of jobs worldwide, benefiting local economies and communities.

Developing domestic supply chains for renewable energy technologies can further enhance these economic benefits. By investing in local manufacturing and assembly facilities, governments can create high-quality jobs, stimulate innovation, and foster industrial growth. These efforts not only boost economic resilience but also ensure that the benefits of the renewable energy transition are distributed equitably.

Promoting Sustainability and Ethical Practices

Sustainable and ethical supply chains are vital for minimizing the environmental and social impacts of renewable energy production. The extraction and processing of raw materials for renewable energy technologies can have significant environmental consequences, including habitat destruction, water pollution, and greenhouse gas emissions. Similarly, labor practices in some regions have raised concerns about exploitation and unsafe working conditions.

Policymakers and businesses must prioritize sustainability and ethical practices throughout the supply chain. This includes adopting environmentally responsible mining practices, reducing waste and emissions, and ensuring fair labor standards. Certification programs and international agreements can help establish guidelines and benchmarks for sustainable and ethical supply chain management.

Addressing Supply Chain Vulnerabilities

Despite their importance, renewable energy supply chains face several vulnerabilities that must be addressed to ensure reliability and resilience. These include resource scarcity, market concentration, and geopolitical tensions. For example, the production of key materials such as lithium and cobalt is concentrated in a few countries, creating risks of supply shortages and price volatility. Policymakers must work to diversify supply sources, develop recycling and circular economy initiatives, and invest in alternative materials to reduce dependency on critical resources.

Technological innovation also plays a crucial role in strengthening renewable energy supply chains. Advances in materials science, manufacturing processes, and digital technologies can improve efficiency, reduce costs, and enhance transparency throughout the supply chain. For instance, blockchain technology can be used to track the provenance of materials, ensuring compliance with sustainability and ethical standards.

Addressing Vulnerabilities in Renewable Energy Supply Chains

The reliability and resilience of renewable energy supply chains are critical to achieving a sustainable energy future. However, these supply chains face various vulnerabilities that can hinder the deployment and integration of renewable energy technologies. These vulnerabilities include resource scarcity, market concentration, geopolitical risks, and disruptions caused by global events such as pandemics or natural disasters. Addressing these challenges requires a coordinated effort by policymakers, businesses, and other stakeholders to ensure that renewable energy systems are robust, reliable, and capable of meeting growing demand.

Resource Scarcity and Critical Materials

Renewable energy technologies depend on critical materials, such as lithium, cobalt, nickel, and rare earth elements, which are essential for components like batteries, solar panels, and wind turbines. However, the availability of these materials is limited, and their extraction often poses environmental and social challenges. For example, the mining of cobalt, a key component of lithium-ion batteries, has raised concerns about environmental degradation and unethical labor practices in some regions.

To address resource scarcity, policymakers and businesses must invest in alternative materials and technologies that reduce dependency on critical resources. For example, advancements in battery technology, such as solid-state batteries or sodium-ion batteries, can help mitigate the demand for materials like cobalt and lithium. Additionally, promoting recycling and the circular economy can extend the lifespan of materials and reduce the need for new extraction. Establishing robust recycling systems for renewable energy components, such as end-of-life solar panels and wind turbine blades, can recover valuable materials and minimize waste.

Market Concentration and Supply Chain Bottlenecks

The production and processing of critical materials are often concentrated in a few countries, creating risks of supply chain bottlenecks and price volatility. For instance, China dominates the global supply chain for rare earth elements, while a significant portion of cobalt production is concentrated in the Democratic Republic of Congo. This reliance on a small number of suppliers increases vulnerability to geopolitical tensions, trade restrictions, and other disruptions.

Diversifying supply sources is essential to reducing these risks. Policymakers can encourage domestic production and processing of critical materials by providing incentives for mining and refining operations. For example, governments can invest in infrastructure, offer tax benefits, and streamline permitting processes to attract investments in local supply chains. International collaboration is also critical, as countries can work together to develop shared resources, establish trade agreements, and create global supply networks.

Geopolitical Risks and Trade Barriers

Geopolitical tensions and trade barriers can significantly impact the availability and cost of renewable energy components. For example, trade disputes or sanctions may restrict access to critical materials, while tariffs on renewable energy technologies can increase costs for developers and consumers. Addressing these risks requires proactive diplomacy and strategic policymaking.

Policymakers should prioritize international cooperation and trade agreements that promote open and fair markets for renewable energy components. Multilateral agreements, such as those facilitated by the World Trade Organization, can help reduce tariffs and ensure stable trade relationships. Additionally, fostering regional partnerships, such as those within the European Union or the African Continental Free Trade Area, can strengthen supply chain resilience by pooling resources and expertise.

Infrastructure Limitations

The infrastructure required to support renewable energy supply chains is often inadequate, particularly in developing countries. Insufficient transportation networks, port facilities, and energy infrastructure can create bottlenecks and delays in the delivery of renewable energy components. For instance, remote locations with abundant renewable energy potential, such as offshore wind farms or desert solar installations, may lack the necessary infrastructure to connect to the grid or transport components.

Investing in infrastructure development is essential to addressing these limitations. Governments should prioritize the construction of roads, railways, and ports to facilitate the efficient movement of renewable energy components. Additionally, upgrading energy infrastructure, such as transmission lines and storage facilities, can ensure the smooth integration of renewable energy systems into existing grids. Public-private partnerships can play a key role in financing and implementing infrastructure projects, leveraging the expertise and resources of both sectors.

Disruptions from Global Events

Global events such as pandemics, natural disasters, or economic crises can disrupt renewable energy supply chains, leading to delays, increased costs, and reduced availability of components. For example, the COVID-19 pandemic caused widespread disruptions in manufacturing and logistics, delaying renewable energy projects worldwide. Similarly, extreme weather events, such as hurricanes or floods, can damage infrastructure and interrupt supply chains.

Building resilience to global disruptions requires proactive risk management and contingency planning. Policymakers and businesses should develop strategies to anticipate and mitigate the impact of potential disruptions. For instance, maintaining strategic reserves of critical materials, diversifying transportation routes, and establishing redundant supply networks can help ensure continuity during crises. Additionally, incorporating digital technologies, such as blockchain and real-time tracking systems, can enhance supply chain transparency and improve responsiveness to disruptions.

Promoting Sustainability and Ethical Practices

The environmental and social impacts of renewable energy supply chains must also be addressed to ensure their long-term sustainability. The extraction and processing of critical materials often result in environmental degradation, such as deforestation, water pollution, and greenhouse gas emissions. Additionally, unethical labor practices, including child labor and unsafe working conditions, are prevalent in some mining operations.

To address these issues, policymakers and businesses should implement and enforce sustainability and ethical standards throughout the supply chain. Certification programs, such as the Initiative for Responsible Mining Assurance (IRMA) or the Responsible Cobalt Initiative, can help ensure compliance with environmental and social criteria. Governments can also establish regulations that mandate sustainable practices, such as requiring renewable energy developers to source materials from certified suppliers. Transparency and accountability are key, as consumers and investors increasingly demand products that meet high ethical and environmental standards.

Advancing Technology and Innovation

Technological innovation plays a critical role in addressing vulnerabilities in renewable energy supply chains. Advances in materials science, manufacturing processes, and digital tools can improve efficiency, reduce costs, and enhance resilience. For example, 3D printing can enable on-demand production of renewable energy components, reducing dependency on complex supply chains. Similarly, artificial intelligence and machine learning can optimize supply chain operations, predict demand, and identify potential risks.

Investing in research and development is essential to driving innovation. Governments, businesses, and academic institutions should collaborate to advance technologies that address supply chain challenges. Public funding, tax incentives, and partnerships with private sector entities can accelerate the development and deployment of innovative solutions.

Localizing Supply Chains for Security

Localizing renewable energy supply chains is essential for enhancing energy security, reducing dependency on global markets, and fostering economic resilience. Renewable energy technologies, such as solar panels, wind turbines, and energy storage systems, rely on complex supply chains often spanning multiple countries. While global trade has enabled rapid advancements in renewable energy deployment, it has also exposed supply chains to risks such as geopolitical tensions, trade disruptions, and global crises. By developing localized supply chains, nations can strengthen their energy independence and build a more secure and sustainable renewable energy sector.

Reducing Dependency on Imports

Many renewable energy components, such as solar cells, wind turbine blades, and batteries, are manufactured in a few key regions, creating dependency on imports for countries without domestic production capabilities. For instance, China dominates the global production of photovoltaic cells and rare earth elements critical for wind turbines and energy storage. This reliance on imports makes countries vulnerable to supply chain disruptions caused by trade disputes, tariffs, or export restrictions.

Localizing supply chains helps mitigate these risks by reducing reliance on foreign suppliers. By fostering domestic production of renewable energy components, countries can ensure a steady and reliable supply of materials and technologies. This not only enhances energy security but also reduces exposure to price volatility in global markets. For example, establishing local manufacturing facilities for solar panels or wind turbines can stabilize costs and minimize delays in project development.

Strengthening Economic Resilience

Developing localized renewable energy supply chains contributes to economic resilience by stimulating industrial growth and creating high-quality jobs. Domestic production of renewable energy components supports local economies by generating employment opportunities in manufacturing, assembly, and maintenance. Additionally, it fosters innovation and technology transfer, enabling countries to build expertise in renewable energy technologies.

Investments in local supply chains can also provide long-term economic benefits by reducing trade deficits associated with importing energy technologies. For example, countries that produce their own renewable energy components can retain more value within their economies, reinvesting profits into research, infrastructure, and workforce development. This economic self-reliance strengthens resilience to external shocks and promotes sustainable growth.

Enhancing Supply Chain Transparency

Localizing supply chains improves transparency and accountability in the sourcing and production of renewable energy components. Global supply chains often involve multiple intermediaries, making it difficult to track the origins of materials and ensure compliance with environmental and ethical standards. For instance, concerns about unethical labor practices in cobalt mining or the environmental impact of rare earth extraction have highlighted the need for greater oversight in global supply chains.

By localizing production, countries can implement stricter regulations and monitoring mechanisms to ensure that renewable energy components meet high environmental and social standards. This includes promoting sustainable mining practices, reducing waste and emissions, and enforcing fair labor conditions. Enhanced transparency not only builds consumer trust but also aligns supply chain practices with broader sustainability goals.

Addressing Regional Resource Availability

Localized supply chains can leverage regional resource availability to optimize production and reduce transportation costs. For example, countries with abundant natural resources, such as silicon for solar panels or lithium for batteries, can develop domestic industries that capitalize on these advantages. This approach minimizes the environmental footprint of supply chains by reducing the need for long-distance transportation and associated carbon emissions.

In regions with limited natural resources, localized supply chains can focus on manufacturing, assembly, and recycling processes. Establishing recycling facilities for renewable energy components, such as end-of-life solar panels or wind turbines, can recover valuable materials and reduce dependence on raw material imports. These efforts contribute to a circular economy, extending the lifecycle of materials and reducing waste.

Building Resilience to Global Disruptions

Global events such as pandemics, natural disasters, or geopolitical conflicts can disrupt international supply chains, causing delays and shortages in renewable energy components. For example, the COVID-19 pandemic highlighted vulnerabilities in global supply networks, leading to delays in solar panel and battery shipments. Localizing supply chains provides a buffer against such disruptions by ensuring that critical components are produced and distributed domestically.

Policymakers can support supply chain localization by investing in infrastructure, offering financial incentives, and fostering partnerships between governments, businesses, and research institutions. For instance, public funding for local manufacturing facilities or tax incentives for renewable energy companies can encourage domestic production. Collaboration with universities and technical institutes can also enhance workforce training and innovation, ensuring that local industries remain competitive in the global market.

Chapter 4: Building a Skilled Workforce for Renewables

The transition to renewable energy is not only a technological and economic challenge but also a human one. A skilled workforce is critical to designing, installing, maintaining, and innovating renewable energy systems. From wind turbine technicians and solar panel installers to engineers and project managers, the renewable energy sector requires diverse expertise across a wide range of disciplines. However, the rapid growth of this sector has outpaced the availability of trained professionals, creating a skills gap that must be addressed to ensure the success of the global energy transition.

This chapter explores the importance of workforce development in the renewable energy industry, examining the key skills and training programs needed to meet the demands of this growing sector. It highlights the challenges of reskilling workers from traditional energy industries, the role of educational institutions in providing specialized training, and the need for inclusive workforce policies that promote diversity and equity. By investing in workforce development, countries can not only accelerate the adoption of renewable energy but also create high-quality jobs, drive innovation, and support long-term economic growth. This chapter provides a roadmap for policymakers, industry leaders, and educators to build a workforce capable of powering the renewable energy future.

Skills Required for the Renewable Energy Sector

The renewable energy sector is one of the fastest-growing industries globally, driving significant demand for a skilled workforce capable of supporting its rapid expansion. From technical expertise to management and policy development, the industry requires a diverse range of skills to ensure the efficient deployment, operation, and maintenance of renewable energy technologies. As the sector continues to evolve, the ability to adapt and acquire new competencies will be essential for workers and organizations alike.

Technical Skills

Technical skills form the backbone of the renewable energy workforce. These include the knowledge and expertise required to install, operate, and maintain renewable energy systems such as solar panels, wind turbines, hydropower plants, and energy storage systems. For example, solar panel installers need proficiency in electrical systems, wiring, and system integration, while wind turbine technicians require expertise in mechanical systems, blade repair, and turbine maintenance.

Advances in technology have also introduced a need for specialized technical skills, such as those related to energy storage systems and smart grids. Battery technicians, for instance, must understand battery chemistry, energy management systems, and safety protocols to ensure the reliable performance of storage solutions. Similarly, grid engineers must be skilled in designing and maintaining smart grid infrastructure to facilitate the integration of variable renewable energy sources into existing networks.

Engineering and Design

The renewable energy sector relies heavily on engineers to design, optimize, and innovate energy systems. Electrical, mechanical, and civil engineers play a critical role in developing technologies such as wind turbines, solar modules, and hydropower systems. For instance, mechanical engineers may focus on improving the aerodynamics of wind turbine blades, while civil engineers design the foundations and structural supports for large-scale solar farms.

Software and systems engineers are also increasingly in demand as renewable energy systems become more digitized. These professionals develop algorithms, control systems, and software platforms that optimize energy generation, storage, and distribution. Expertise in fields such as artificial intelligence and machine learning is particularly valuable for creating predictive maintenance systems and enhancing grid performance.

Project Management and Planning

Project management is another essential skill set in the renewable energy industry. Managers and planners are responsible for overseeing the lifecycle of renewable energy projects, from feasibility studies and permitting to construction and commissioning. This requires a combination of organizational, financial, and technical knowledge to ensure projects are completed on time, within budget, and in compliance with regulatory requirements.

Key skills in this area include risk management, stakeholder engagement, and familiarity with renewable energy financing models such as PPAs and green bonds. Project managers must also navigate complex supply chains, coordinate multidisciplinary teams, and address logistical challenges to ensure the successful implementation of renewable energy projects.

Policy and Regulatory Expertise

The success of renewable energy initiatives depends on favorable policy and regulatory environments. Professionals with expertise in energy policy, environmental regulations, and market design are essential for shaping the frameworks that govern renewable energy development. For example, policy analysts and regulatory specialists work to draft legislation, assess the impact of incentives such as feed-in tariffs, and ensure compliance with international climate agreements.

Knowledge of emissions reduction strategies, carbon markets, and renewable energy certificates is also critical for aligning projects with sustainability goals. Professionals in this field must be adept at conducting policy analysis, engaging with stakeholders, and advocating for policies that promote renewable energy adoption.

Communication and Outreach

Public awareness and acceptance are crucial for the success of renewable energy projects, particularly those involving large-scale infrastructure such as wind farms or solar parks. Communication and outreach professionals play a vital role in educating communities, addressing concerns, and building support for renewable energy initiatives. Skills in public relations, stakeholder engagement, and community consultation are essential for fostering collaboration and reducing opposition to projects.

These professionals also contribute to marketing renewable energy products and services, helping businesses reach new customers and expand their market share. Expertise in digital communication, content creation, and social media strategies is increasingly valuable in this context.

Emerging Skills for a Changing Sector

As the renewable energy sector evolves, new skills are emerging to meet the demands of cutting-edge technologies and practices. For example, expertise in hydrogen production and utilization is becoming increasingly important as green hydrogen gains traction as a renewable energy solution. Similarly, professionals with knowledge of carbon capture and storage (CCS) technologies are needed to complement renewable energy systems and reduce emissions.

Another emerging area is the integration of renewable energy with electric mobility. Professionals skilled in EV charging infrastructure, vehicle-to-grid (V2G) technology, and energy management systems are essential for supporting the growing intersection of renewable energy and transportation.

Strategies for Workforce Development in the Renewable Energy Sector

The rapid expansion of the renewable energy sector requires a skilled and adaptable workforce to meet its growing demands.

Building a workforce capable of supporting this transition involves implementing targeted strategies that address current skill gaps, foster innovation, and ensure inclusivity. Policymakers, industry leaders, and educational institutions must collaborate to design programs and initiatives that equip workers with the knowledge and expertise needed to support the growth of renewable energy technologies. This chapter explores key strategies for workforce development, emphasizing training, education, reskilling, and capacity building.

Expanding Education and Training Programs

One of the most effective strategies for workforce development is the expansion of education and training programs tailored to the renewable energy sector. These programs must focus on both foundational skills and specialized expertise required for roles in solar, wind, hydropower, and energy storage systems.

Technical and Vocational Education and Training (TVET):

TVET programs play a vital role in equipping workers with the hands-on skills needed for installation, operation, and maintenance of renewable energy technologies. For example, technicians working on solar panels require training in electrical systems, wiring, and troubleshooting, while wind turbine technicians need expertise in mechanical systems and safety protocols. Governments and industries should invest in TVET institutions and ensure that their curricula align with the specific needs of the renewable energy sector.

Higher Education Initiatives:

Universities and colleges must expand their offerings in renewable energy engineering, environmental sciences, and energy management. Interdisciplinary programs that combine technical knowledge with policy, economics, and business skills can prepare students for leadership roles in the industry. Collaboration between academia and the private sector is essential to ensure that graduates are well-prepared for the job market.

Reskilling and Upskilling the Workforce

The transition to renewable energy presents an opportunity to reskill workers from traditional energy industries, such as coal, oil, and gas, to take on roles in the renewable sector. Reskilling programs are essential for mitigating job displacement and ensuring a just transition for affected workers.

Industry-Led Initiatives:

Renewable energy companies can play a significant role in reskilling by offering training programs for workers transitioning from fossil fuel industries. For example, programs can teach former coal plant workers the skills needed to install or maintain wind turbines and solar panels. On-the-job training and apprenticeships are particularly effective in helping workers gain practical experience in new roles.

Government Support for Reskilling:

Policymakers should establish reskilling funds and grants to support workers transitioning into renewable energy jobs. These initiatives can include subsidized training programs, income support during training periods, and incentives for companies that hire reskilled workers. Governments can also partner with labor unions and industry associations to ensure reskilling programs address the needs of displaced workers.

Building Capacity in Emerging Markets

In many developing countries, the lack of a skilled workforce is a significant barrier to renewable energy deployment. Building capacity in these regions is essential for ensuring equitable access to clean energy and supporting global sustainability goals.

Regional Training Centers:

Establishing regional renewable energy training centers can provide workers in developing countries with access to high-quality education and training programs. These centers can focus on skills needed for local renewable energy projects, such as small-scale solar installations or off-grid energy systems. Partnerships with international organizations can provide funding, expertise, and resources for these centers.

Knowledge Transfer Programs:

Developed countries and multinational companies can support workforce development in emerging markets through knowledge transfer programs. These initiatives involve sharing technical expertise, best practices, and training materials with local institutions and workers. For example, renewable energy firms operating in developing countries can partner with local governments to provide training for technicians and engineers.

Promoting Diversity and Inclusion

To fully realize the potential of the renewable energy sector, workforce development strategies must prioritize diversity and inclusion. Women, minorities, and underrepresented groups often face barriers to entry in technical and engineering fields. Addressing these disparities can expand the talent pool and ensure that renewable energy benefits all members of society.

Targeted Outreach and Recruitment:

Policymakers and companies can implement outreach programs that encourage underrepresented groups to pursue careers in renewable energy. Scholarships, mentorship programs, and internships specifically designed for women and minorities can help break down barriers and increase representation in the sector.

Inclusive Workplace Policies:

Renewable energy companies must adopt policies that promote diversity and inclusion in the workplace. This includes providing equal opportunities for hiring and advancement, offering flexible work arrangements, and fostering a supportive work environment. Addressing pay gaps and ensuring equal pay for equal work is also essential for creating an inclusive workforce.

Leveraging Technology for Workforce Development

Advances in technology can enhance workforce development efforts by providing innovative tools for training, education, and skill building. Digital platforms, VR, and artificial intelligence (AI) can make learning more accessible and engaging.

Online Training Platforms:

Online platforms can deliver renewable energy training programs to workers in remote or underserved areas. Courses on solar installation, wind turbine maintenance, and energy efficiency can be made available through e-learning platforms, enabling workers to gain skills at their own pace. Interactive modules and certification programs can further enhance the value of online training.

Virtual Reality for Practical Training:

VR technology can provide immersive training experiences for renewable energy workers, allowing them to practice technical skills in a simulated environment. For example, wind turbine technicians can use VR to simulate working at heights, while solar installers can practice wiring and troubleshooting in virtual setups. These technologies reduce the need for physical training facilities and provide a safe environment for skill development.

Collaboration Between Stakeholders

Effective workforce development requires collaboration between governments, industry leaders, educational institutions, and non-governmental organizations (NGOs). Partnerships between these stakeholders can ensure that training programs align with industry needs, leverage resources efficiently, and reach a broad audience.

Public-Private Partnerships:

Governments can partner with renewable energy companies to fund and implement workforce development programs. For example, public funding can support training centers, while companies provide expertise and equipment for hands-on learning. These partnerships can also facilitate internships and apprenticeships, giving workers valuable real-world experience.

International Collaboration:

Global efforts to develop the renewable energy workforce can be strengthened through international collaboration. Organizations such as the International Renewable Energy Agency (IRENA) and the United Nations can facilitate knowledge sharing, provide funding, and coordinate capacity-building programs across countries. Collaborative initiatives can address global skill shortages and promote equitable workforce development.

Bridging Skill Gaps in the Renewable Energy Sector

The renewable energy sector's rapid expansion has outpaced the availability of skilled workers, resulting in significant skill gaps across various roles. From technical expertise in system installation and maintenance to policy development and project management, the sector requires a diverse range of skills to support its growth. Bridging these skill gaps is essential to meeting renewable energy targets, ensuring system reliability, and driving innovation. A coordinated approach involving governments, educational institutions, and industries is required to equip the workforce with the necessary competencies.

Identifying Key Skill Gaps

Skill gaps in the renewable energy sector arise from both the rapid growth of the industry and the unique requirements of emerging technologies. These gaps can be broadly categorized into technical, managerial, and policy-related areas:

• **Technical Skills:** A shortage of trained technicians and engineers is a significant challenge. For example, solar and wind energy systems require specialized expertise in installation, operation, and maintenance, yet many regions lack adequate training programs to meet this demand. Additionally, skills related to emerging technologies such as energy storage, hydrogen production, and smart grids are increasingly in demand but are not widely available.

• **Managerial Skills:** Effective project management and planning are critical to ensuring the timely and cost-effective completion of renewable energy projects. However, many professionals entering the sector lack experience in managing large-scale infrastructure projects or navigating complex regulatory environments.

• **Policy and Regulatory Skills:** Policymakers and regulators need expertise in designing frameworks that support renewable energy integration. This includes skills in market design, carbon pricing, and policy analysis, which are essential for creating favorable conditions for renewable energy deployment.

Expanding Education and Training Opportunities

Addressing skill gaps begins with expanding access to education and training programs that align with industry needs. Tailored curricula and targeted initiatives can help bridge the gap between the skills workers have and those required by employers.

• **Technical and Vocational Training:** Technical and vocational education and training (TVET) programs are essential for equipping workers with the practical skills needed for renewable energy roles.

These programs should focus on core competencies such as solar panel installation, wind turbine maintenance, and energy system troubleshooting. Governments can support TVET expansion by funding training centers and incentivizing private-sector involvement.

• **Higher Education Programs:** Universities and colleges play a vital role in producing skilled professionals for advanced roles in the renewable energy sector. Programs in renewable energy engineering, environmental sciences, and energy policy should incorporate hands-on experience and industry collaborations to ensure graduates are job-ready.

Reskilling and Upskilling Initiatives

Reskilling and upskilling programs are critical for addressing skill gaps, particularly as workers transition from traditional energy sectors into renewable energy roles. These programs provide opportunities for individuals to acquire new skills or enhance their existing expertise.

• **Targeted Reskilling for Displaced Workers:** Workers from fossil fuel industries, such as coal or oil and gas, possess transferable skills that can be adapted to renewable energy jobs. Reskilling programs should focus on helping these workers transition by providing training in renewable energy technologies and practices. For example, a coal plant operator can be trained to manage wind farm operations or energy storage systems.

• **Continuous Professional Development:** Upskilling programs for existing renewable energy professionals help them stay current with advancements in technology and market trends. Workshops, certifications, and online courses can provide opportunities for professionals to deepen their knowledge and expand their capabilities.

Leveraging Technology for Skills Development

Innovative technologies, such as e-learning platforms and virtual reality (VR), can play a significant role in bridging skill gaps. These tools make training more accessible, flexible, and engaging for learners.

• **E-learning Platforms:** Online platforms offer a cost-effective way to deliver training programs to a wide audience. Workers in remote areas can access courses on solar installation, wind turbine maintenance, and other renewable energy topics without needing to travel. Interactive features, such as quizzes and simulations, enhance the learning experience.

• **Virtual Reality Training:** VR provides immersive training environments where workers can practice technical skills in a risk-free setting. For example, VR can simulate scenarios such as working on wind turbine blades at great heights or troubleshooting solar panel systems, enabling learners to build confidence and competence.

Encouraging Collaboration Among Stakeholders

Bridging skill gaps requires collaboration between governments, industry leaders, and educational institutions. Stakeholders must work together to identify workforce needs, design effective training programs, and ensure alignment with market demands.

• **Public-Private Partnerships:** Governments can partner with renewable energy companies to co-develop training initiatives. For instance, public funding can support the establishment of training centers, while companies provide expertise, equipment, and internship opportunities.

• **Industry-Academia Collaborations:** Universities and colleges can collaborate with industry leaders to design curricula that reflect real-world challenges. Industry experts can deliver guest lectures, mentor students, and offer internships to bridge the gap between education and employment.

Ensuring Inclusivity in Workforce Development

Efforts to bridge skill gaps must prioritize inclusivity to ensure equal access to opportunities in the renewable energy sector. Women, minorities, and underrepresented groups often face barriers to entry, which limits the available talent pool.

• **Diversity Recruitment Programs:** Outreach initiatives that target underrepresented groups can encourage them to pursue careers in renewable energy. Scholarships, mentorship programs, and tailored training courses can help address disparities and expand the talent pool.

• **Accessible Training Programs:** Flexible learning options, such as part-time courses and online training, make it easier for individuals from diverse backgrounds to acquire skills. Ensuring affordability and offering financial support can further enhance access to training opportunities.

Chapter 5: Scaling Up Financing for Renewable Energy

The transition to renewable energy is a capital-intensive endeavor that requires significant investments in infrastructure, technology, and innovation. Scaling up financing is essential to bridge the gap between current funding levels and the investment needed to achieve global renewable energy targets. From utility-scale solar and wind projects to decentralized energy systems in remote areas, the renewable energy sector relies on diverse financing sources to drive deployment and innovation.

This chapter explores the critical role of financing in accelerating the renewable energy transition. It examines the various funding mechanisms available, including public investment, private sector financing, and blended finance models, highlighting their unique advantages and challenges. The chapter also addresses barriers to financing, such as high upfront costs and perceived risks, and provides strategies to overcome them through policy frameworks, incentives, and innovative financial instruments.

By focusing on practical solutions, this chapter aims to equip policymakers, financial institutions, and investors with the tools to scale up financing for renewable energy projects. Ensuring adequate and accessible financing is not only vital for meeting renewable energy goals but also for fostering economic growth, creating jobs, and ensuring energy equity.

The Role of Financial Investment in Renewable Energy

Financial investment plays a pivotal role in driving the global transition to renewable energy. The development, deployment, and scaling of renewable energy technologies require substantial capital, making access to financing critical for achieving ambitious climate and energy goals. Investments in renewable energy contribute not only to decarbonizing energy systems but also to fostering economic growth, creating jobs, and improving energy access.

Enabling Project Development

One of the primary roles of financial investment is to fund the development and implementation of renewable energy projects. Solar farms, wind turbines, hydropower plants, and energy storage systems all require significant upfront capital for planning, permitting, construction, and commissioning. Without adequate investment, many projects would remain conceptual and fail to reach operational status.

Financial investment supports various stages of project development. During the initial phases, funds are needed for feasibility studies, environmental impact assessments, and securing permits. Once the project design is finalized, additional capital is required for procurement of equipment, labor, and construction. For instance, building a utility-scale solar farm involves significant costs for solar panels, inverters, and mounting structures. Investment ensures these resources are available to complete the project.

Driving Technological Innovation

Investment is also crucial for advancing renewable energy technologies. Research and development (R&D) efforts are needed to improve the efficiency, reliability, and cost-effectiveness of renewable energy systems. For example, innovations in photovoltaic cell technology have significantly increased the efficiency of solar panels while reducing their production costs. Similarly, advancements in wind turbine design have improved energy output and expanded the viability of wind power in lower-wind-speed regions.

Private and public investments in R&D accelerate the commercialization of emerging technologies, such as energy storage solutions, green hydrogen, and floating offshore wind. These innovations address key challenges in the renewable energy sector, such as intermittency and grid integration, enabling broader adoption of clean energy systems.

Supporting Infrastructure Expansion

Financial investment plays a vital role in expanding the infrastructure needed to integrate renewable energy into existing energy systems. Upgrading transmission and distribution networks is essential to accommodate the variable nature of renewable energy sources. For example, wind farms are often located in remote areas far from population centers, requiring extensive transmission lines to deliver electricity to consumers.

Investments in energy storage infrastructure, such as battery systems, are also critical for managing fluctuations in renewable energy generation and ensuring grid stability. Additionally, decentralized energy systems, such as microgrids and rooftop solar, require financial backing to develop the necessary infrastructure for local energy production and distribution.

Attracting Private Sector Participation

Private sector participation is essential to mobilizing the large-scale investments needed for the renewable energy transition. Governments and public institutions alone cannot meet the financial requirements of the sector, making it necessary to attract private capital through innovative financing mechanisms. Financial investments act as a catalyst, reducing risks and incentivizing private companies to enter the renewable energy market.

Public-private partnerships (PPPs) are an effective model for leveraging private sector resources. In these arrangements, governments provide initial funding, policy support, and guarantees, while private investors contribute capital and expertise. For example, governments may offer subsidies or tax incentives to reduce financial risks and make renewable energy projects more attractive to private investors.

Enhancing Energy Equity

Financial investment also plays a critical role in ensuring energy equity by funding projects in underserved and marginalized communities. Renewable energy has the potential to bring electricity to remote and rural areas that lack access to centralized energy systems. Investments in decentralized renewable energy solutions, such as mini-grids and standalone solar systems, can bridge the energy access gap, improving quality of life and fostering economic development.

International financial institutions, development banks, and philanthropic organizations are instrumental in funding renewable energy projects in developing countries. These investments often include concessional loans, grants, or technical assistance to reduce financial barriers and ensure that the benefits of renewable energy reach vulnerable populations.

Overcoming Financial Barriers

Despite the growing importance of renewable energy, several financial barriers hinder its deployment. High upfront costs, perceived risks, and limited access to capital are common challenges faced by project developers and investors. Financial investment can address these barriers by offering solutions such as long-term financing, risk mitigation instruments, and blended finance models.

Blended finance, which combines public and private funding, is particularly effective in de-risking renewable energy projects. By using public funds to absorb initial risks, blended finance models encourage private sector participation and unlock additional capital. Instruments such as green bonds, credit guarantees, and PPAs further enhance the financial viability of renewable energy projects.

Key Financing Sources for Renewable Energy: Public, Private, and Blended

The transition to renewable energy is a capital-intensive endeavor requiring diverse financing sources to meet global energy goals. Financing can broadly be categorized into public, private, and blended sources, each playing a critical role in supporting the development, deployment, and scaling of renewable energy technologies. While public financing establishes the foundational support needed for early-stage projects and risk mitigation, private investment drives large-scale deployment and innovation. Blended financing combines these approaches, leveraging the strengths of both to mobilize additional capital. This chapter examines the contributions, challenges, and synergies of these three financing sources.

Public Financing: Catalyzing Renewable Energy Development

Public financing is a cornerstone of renewable energy investment, particularly in the early stages of project development. Governments, development banks, and international institutions provide the funding needed to reduce financial risks, enable innovation, and promote equitable access to clean energy. Public financing often takes the form of direct funding, subsidies, concessional loans, or grants.

Role of Governments:

Governments play a critical role in financing renewable energy projects, especially in areas where private sector participation is limited. Public funds are used to establish incentives, such as FiTs, ITCs, and PTCs, which lower the financial barriers to renewable energy adoption. These measures create a stable and predictable policy environment, encouraging private investment.

Public financing also supports R&D in renewable energy technologies, driving innovation and cost reductions. For instance, government-funded R&D programs have contributed significantly to advancements in solar panel efficiency and wind turbine technology. Infrastructure development, such as upgrading grid systems or establishing transmission lines for remote wind farms, is another area where public funds are essential.

Role of Development Banks:

Multilateral and bilateral development banks, such as the World Bank, Asian Development Bank, and African Development Bank, are vital sources of public financing for renewable energy in developing countries. These institutions provide concessional loans and technical assistance to support renewable energy projects that may not attract private investors due to high risks or low returns. For example, development banks often fund off-grid solar systems in rural areas, bringing clean energy to underserved populations.

Private Financing: Driving Innovation and Scale

Private sector financing is the engine that drives large-scale deployment and technological innovation in renewable energy. Investment from private entities, including corporations, institutional investors, venture capitalists, and individuals, accounts for the majority of global renewable energy financing.

Corporate Investments:

Energy companies, utilities, and independent power producers (IPPs) are key players in the renewable energy market. These entities invest in large-scale solar farms, wind projects, and energy storage systems to diversify their portfolios and meet regulatory or corporate sustainability goals. For example, utility companies may develop renewable energy projects to comply with renewable portfolio standards (RPS) or to transition away from fossil fuels.

Institutional Investors:

Pension funds, insurance companies, and sovereign wealth funds are increasingly allocating capital to renewable energy projects due to their long-term investment horizons and stable returns. Green bonds, which finance environmentally sustainable projects, have become a popular instrument for institutional investors, raising billions of dollars for renewable energy initiatives globally.

Venture Capital and Private Equity:

Venture capital (VC) and private equity (PE) firms play a significant role in supporting early-stage companies and emerging technologies in the renewable energy sector. For instance, VC firms often fund startups developing innovative solutions in energy storage, smart grids, or hydrogen production. While these investments carry higher risks, they also offer the potential for substantial returns.

Challenges for Private Financing:

Private financing is not without challenges. High upfront costs, long payback periods, and perceived risks, such as regulatory uncertainty or market volatility, can deter private investors. To address these concerns, governments and public institutions often step in with risk mitigation mechanisms, such as guarantees or insurance, to encourage private sector participation.

Blended Financing: Mobilizing Additional Capital

Blended financing combines public and private funding to leverage the strengths of both sources and mobilize additional capital for renewable energy projects. This approach is particularly effective in addressing high-risk projects or those in developing markets, where private investment may be limited.

Public-Private Partnerships:

PPPs are a common model of blended financing, where governments and private companies collaborate on renewable energy projects. In this arrangement, the public sector typically provides initial funding, guarantees, or policy support, while the private sector contributes capital, expertise, and project management. For example, a PPP might fund the construction of a wind farm, with the government guaranteeing a minimum price for the electricity generated.

Concessional Finance:

Concessional finance refers to loans or grants provided by public institutions at below-market rates to reduce the financial risks of renewable energy projects. These funds are often combined with private capital to make projects more attractive to investors. For instance, concessional loans might cover the initial costs of a solar farm, while private investors finance its long-term operations.

Green Climate Fund (GCF):

The Green Climate Fund is an example of a blended financing mechanism designed to support renewable energy and climate resilience projects in developing countries. The GCF provides grants, loans, equity, and guarantees to de-risk projects and attract private sector participation. By sharing risks, the GCF enables large-scale investments that would otherwise not be feasible.

Advantages of Blended Financing:

Blended financing offers several advantages, including risk reduction, scalability, and inclusivity. By combining public funds with private capital, this approach mobilizes significantly more resources than either source could provide independently. It also ensures that projects in high-risk or underserved areas receive adequate funding.

The Synergy Between Sources

While public, private, and blended financing sources each have unique strengths, their combined use creates a synergistic effect that accelerates the renewable energy transition. Public financing lays the groundwork by funding R&D, infrastructure, and policy support. Private financing drives innovation and large-scale deployment, while blended financing bridges gaps, enabling projects that might otherwise face financial barriers.

For example, a government might provide tax incentives and regulatory support for a wind farm, while private investors fund construction and operations. Development banks could step in with concessional loans to de-risk the project, creating a collaborative financing structure that ensures success.

Policies to Attract Investment in Renewable Energy

Attracting investment in renewable energy is critical to meeting global energy and climate goals. Policymakers play a key role in creating the conditions that encourage both public and private capital to flow into renewable energy projects. Well-designed policies reduce risks, provide financial incentives, and establish clear frameworks for long-term planning, all of which are essential for fostering investor confidence. This chapter explores the policies that can attract investment and accelerate the deployment of renewable energy technologies.

Establishing Clear and Ambitious Targets

Setting clear and ambitious renewable energy targets is one of the most effective ways to attract investment. Targets, such as achieving a specific percentage of renewable energy generation by a given year, provide a roadmap for the industry and signal a strong commitment to clean energy. These goals give investors confidence in the stability and growth potential of the renewable energy market. For example, countries with legally binding renewable portfolio standards (RPS) often see increased private-sector interest due to the predictable demand for renewable energy.

Interim milestones within these targets can further enhance their effectiveness by allowing investors to track progress and adjust their strategies. Additionally, aligning targets with international agreements, such as the Paris Agreement, reinforces credibility and demonstrates a commitment to global climate goals.

Providing Financial Incentives

Financial incentives are a powerful tool for attracting investment in renewable energy. These policies directly reduce the cost of developing, deploying, and operating renewable energy projects, making them more attractive to investors.

• **Tax Incentives:** Tax credits, exemptions, and deductions lower the financial burden on renewable energy developers. For instance, ITCs allow investors to deduct a percentage of their project costs from their tax liabilities, while PTCs reward renewable energy producers for the electricity they generate.

• **FiTs:** FiTs guarantee fixed payments to renewable energy producers for the electricity they supply to the grid. By ensuring stable and predictable revenue, FiTs reduce market uncertainty and encourage long-term investments.

• **Subsidies and Grants:** Direct subsidies and grants provide upfront capital to offset project development costs, particularly in high-risk or underserved markets. These incentives are especially effective in supporting small-scale or community-based renewable energy projects.

Mitigating Risks

Perceived risks, such as regulatory uncertainty, market volatility, and technology reliability, often deter investors from committing to renewable energy projects. Policymakers can implement risk mitigation mechanisms to address these concerns and create a more favorable investment climate.

• **Power Purchase Agreements:** PPAs provide long-term contracts between renewable energy producers and buyers, guaranteeing a fixed price for the electricity generated. This reduces revenue uncertainty and secures financial returns for investors.

• **Loan Guarantees:** Government-backed loan guarantees lower the risk of default for lenders, encouraging financial institutions to provide capital for renewable energy projects.

• **Carbon Pricing:** Policies such as carbon taxes or cap-and-trade systems internalize the environmental costs of fossil fuel use, making renewable energy more competitive and attractive to investors.

Streamlining Permitting and Regulatory Processes

Complex and lengthy permitting processes can delay renewable energy projects and increase costs, discouraging investment. Streamlining these processes is essential to creating an efficient and predictable regulatory environment.

• **Simplified Permitting:** Establishing standardized permitting procedures for renewable energy projects reduces administrative burdens and accelerates project timelines. For instance, governments can implement one-stop-shop systems where developers can complete all permitting steps through a single agency.

• **Grid Access Rules:** Clear and transparent regulations for grid interconnection ensure that renewable energy producers can connect to the grid without facing excessive delays or costs. Policies that prioritize renewable energy integration, such as guaranteed grid access or priority dispatch, further enhance investor confidence.

Enhancing Policy Stability and Transparency

Stable and transparent policy environments are critical for attracting long-term investment. Frequent policy changes or unclear regulations create uncertainty, deterring investors from committing to renewable energy projects.

• **Long-Term Policy Frameworks:** Developing long-term strategies and commitments for renewable energy ensures consistency and reduces uncertainty. For example, setting multi-decade renewable energy targets provides a stable foundation for investment planning.

• **Transparency in Policy Design:** Policymakers should engage stakeholders, including investors and industry representatives, in the development of renewable energy policies. Open consultation processes and clear communication about policy objectives and timelines enhance trust and reduce ambiguity.

Promoting Public-Private Partnerships

PPPs combine the strengths of public and private sectors to mobilize resources and share risks. Policymakers can facilitate PPPs by offering financial support, regulatory incentives, and guarantees that attract private investment. For example, governments can co-finance renewable energy projects, provide land for development, or guarantee minimum electricity prices to reduce market risks.

Equitable Distribution of Financial Resources

The equitable distribution of financial resources is essential for ensuring that the benefits of renewable energy reach all segments of society, particularly marginalized and underserved communities. While renewable energy offers the potential for environmental sustainability and economic development, access to financing often remains concentrated in wealthier regions, large corporations, and urban centers. Bridging this gap requires targeted policies and innovative financing mechanisms that prioritize inclusivity and fairness.

Addressing Regional Disparities

Access to financial resources for renewable energy projects is often unevenly distributed across regions. Wealthier countries and urban areas typically attract more investment due to their established infrastructure, regulatory stability, and market potential. In contrast, rural and remote areas, particularly in developing countries, often lack the financial resources needed to develop renewable energy systems. These regions face higher risks, inadequate infrastructure, and limited investor interest, which exacerbate energy access disparities.

Policymakers can address regional disparities by allocating public funds to support renewable energy projects in underserved areas. National governments and international organizations should prioritize financing for projects that provide energy access to remote and rural communities. For example, concessional loans and grants can help fund decentralized renewable energy solutions, such as solar mini-grids or standalone systems, which are well-suited to areas lacking centralized grid infrastructure.

Supporting Small-Scale Developers and Communities

Large-scale renewable energy projects often dominate investment flows, leaving small-scale developers and community-led initiatives struggling to secure funding. Yet, these smaller projects play a vital role in diversifying energy sources, enhancing energy resilience, and promoting local economic development. Ensuring that small-scale projects receive equitable financial support is crucial for fostering inclusive growth in the renewable energy sector.

Microfinance and community-based funding models can empower local developers and communities to participate in the renewable energy transition. For example, revolving loan funds and credit cooperatives can provide low-interest loans to small-scale developers, enabling them to finance solar installations or wind projects. Crowdfunding platforms also offer an innovative way for communities to pool resources and invest in renewable energy projects that directly benefit them.

Enhancing Financial Inclusion

Financial exclusion remains a significant barrier for low-income households and small businesses seeking to adopt renewable energy technologies. Many lack access to traditional banking services or credit, making it difficult to finance the upfront costs of solar panels, batteries, or energy-efficient appliances. Addressing this challenge requires innovative financial products that cater to the needs of underserved populations.

Pay-as-you-go (PAYG) models are a successful example of enhancing financial inclusion in the renewable energy sector. These systems allow users to pay for renewable energy services in small, manageable installments, reducing the burden of upfront costs. PAYG models have been particularly effective in regions like sub-Saharan Africa, where they have expanded access to clean energy for millions of off-grid households.

Additionally, financial literacy programs can help individuals and communities understand the benefits of renewable energy and the financing options available to them. By improving financial literacy, policymakers and organizations can empower underserved populations to make informed decisions about adopting renewable energy technologies.

Gender Equality in Financing

Gender inequality is another critical issue in the equitable distribution of financial resources. Women, particularly in developing countries, often face greater barriers to accessing credit and financial services, limiting their ability to invest in renewable energy solutions. Yet, women are key stakeholders in energy transitions, often managing household energy use and contributing to community development.

Policymakers and financial institutions must adopt gender-sensitive approaches to financing. This includes designing financial products tailored to women's needs, such as microloans for female entrepreneurs or targeted subsidies for women-led renewable energy projects. Engaging women in decision-making processes and providing training opportunities can further promote gender equality in the renewable energy sector.

Bridging the Public-Private Divide

Equitable distribution of financial resources requires coordinated efforts between public and private sectors. Public financing plays a vital role in de-risking renewable energy projects and attracting private investment to underserved areas. For instance, blended finance models combine public funds with private capital to mobilize additional resources for projects in high-risk or low-income regions.

Development banks and international organizations can act as intermediaries, channeling funds from high-income countries to support renewable energy initiatives in developing nations. These institutions can also provide technical assistance and capacity building to ensure that financial resources are used effectively and sustainably.

Financing Barriers in Developing Nations

The transition to renewable energy presents significant challenges for developing nations, where access to financing remains a critical barrier. Despite the immense potential of renewable energy to drive sustainable development, many countries face obstacles in mobilizing the financial resources needed to support large-scale adoption. High upfront costs, limited access to credit, and a lack of investment-ready projects are just some of the hurdles that slow progress. Overcoming these barriers is essential to ensuring that developing nations can participate in the global energy transition and achieve energy equity.

High Upfront Costs

One of the most significant financing barriers in developing nations is the high upfront cost of renewable energy technologies. Solar panels, wind turbines, and energy storage systems require substantial initial investment, which is often beyond the reach of governments, businesses, and households in low-income regions. While the long-term benefits of renewable energy, such as reduced energy costs and environmental sustainability, are well-documented, the upfront expenditure remains a major deterrent.

To address this issue, financial institutions and governments must develop mechanisms to spread the cost of renewable energy investments over time. For example, concessional loans with low interest rates and long repayment periods can make renewable energy projects more affordable. Similarly, pay-as-you-go (PAYG) financing models allow households and businesses to pay for renewable energy technologies in small, manageable installments, reducing the burden of upfront costs.

Limited Access to Credit

Access to credit is another major obstacle for renewable energy adoption in developing nations. Many small businesses, households, and even governments lack access to affordable financing options, making it difficult to fund renewable energy projects. In rural areas, where energy access is often most needed, the lack of banking infrastructure and financial services exacerbates this issue.

Microfinance institutions and community-based credit schemes can play a vital role in bridging this gap. By offering small loans to individuals and businesses, these institutions enable the financing of off-grid renewable energy systems, such as solar home systems or mini-grids. Additionally, financial inclusion initiatives that expand access to banking services in underserved areas can help create a more supportive environment for renewable energy investment.

Perceived Investment Risks

Renewable energy projects in developing nations are often perceived as high-risk investments by both domestic and international financiers. Factors such as political instability, regulatory uncertainty, and currency fluctuations contribute to this perception, making it challenging to attract private sector investment. Additionally, many developing nations lack strong legal and institutional frameworks to protect investors, further deterring capital flows.

To mitigate these risks, governments and development institutions can implement risk-sharing mechanisms that provide greater security for investors. For instance, partial risk guarantees or insurance programs can protect investors from losses due to political or economic instability. Establishing stable and transparent regulatory frameworks is also critical for reducing uncertainty and building investor confidence.

Lack of Investment-Ready Projects

Many developing nations face a shortage of investment-ready renewable energy projects, which limits their ability to attract financing. Projects often fail to reach the required level of technical and financial preparation, making them unattractive to potential investors. Challenges include incomplete feasibility studies, unclear business models, and insufficient project management capacity.

Capacity-building programs can help address this issue by equipping local developers with the skills and resources needed to prepare high-quality project proposals. International organizations and development banks can also provide technical assistance to support project preparation, including conducting feasibility studies, designing business plans, and navigating permitting processes.

Inadequate Policy and Regulatory Frameworks

Weak or inconsistent policy and regulatory frameworks are a common barrier to renewable energy financing in developing nations. In some cases, energy policies may prioritize fossil fuel subsidies or fail to provide incentives for renewable energy development. Additionally, unclear or cumbersome permitting processes can delay projects and increase costs.

Policymakers must prioritize the creation of robust policy environments that encourage renewable energy investment. This includes introducing incentives such as feed-in tariffs, tax breaks, or renewable energy credits, as well as streamlining permitting and interconnection procedures. Clear, long-term policies that align with international climate goals can further enhance investor confidence.

Insufficient Public Funding

Public funding is often limited in developing nations, constraining their ability to finance large-scale renewable energy projects or provide subsidies for small-scale systems. Many governments face competing priorities, such as healthcare, education, and infrastructure development, which divert resources away from renewable energy initiatives.

International development assistance and climate finance play a critical role in addressing this funding gap. Initiatives such as the GCF and the Climate Investment Funds (CIF) provide financial support to developing nations for renewable energy projects. These funds often combine grants, concessional loans, and guarantees to reduce financial barriers and catalyze private sector investment.

Lack of Local Manufacturing and Supply Chains

The reliance on imported renewable energy components, such as solar panels or wind turbines, increases costs and delays for projects in developing nations. Many countries lack the manufacturing capacity and supply chain infrastructure needed to produce renewable energy technologies locally, making them dependent on international suppliers.

Investing in local manufacturing and supply chains can help reduce costs, create jobs, and accelerate the deployment of renewable energy. Governments can support this process by offering incentives for renewable energy companies to establish local production facilities, as well as by investing in workforce development to build the necessary skills.

Limited Awareness and Advocacy

In some developing nations, limited awareness of the benefits and opportunities of renewable energy hinders investment and adoption. Many communities and businesses are unfamiliar with renewable energy technologies or lack information about financing options and potential cost savings.

Public awareness campaigns and education initiatives can help bridge this gap. By highlighting the economic, environmental, and social benefits of renewable energy, these efforts can build demand for clean energy solutions. Additionally, engaging local leaders and community organizations can enhance advocacy efforts and encourage broader adoption.

Innovative Financing Mechanisms for Renewable Energy

Innovative financing mechanisms are essential for addressing the financial barriers that hinder the widespread adoption of renewable energy. Traditional funding models often struggle to meet the sector's unique demands, such as high upfront costs, long payback periods, and perceived risks. By leveraging creative financial tools and structures, stakeholders can mobilize capital, reduce risk, and make renewable energy projects more accessible to a diverse range of investors. This chapter explores some of the most impactful innovative financing mechanisms, including green bonds, blended finance, pay-as-you-go models, crowdfunding, and energy-as-a-service models.

Green Bonds

Green bonds are debt instruments specifically designed to finance environmentally sustainable projects, including renewable energy initiatives. These bonds attract institutional and individual investors seeking socially responsible investment opportunities, offering a dual benefit of financial returns and positive environmental impact.

The appeal of green bonds lies in their ability to raise large-scale capital at relatively low interest rates. Governments, corporations, and development banks issue green bonds to fund renewable energy projects such as solar farms, wind parks, and energy storage systems. For example, the European Investment Bank and the World Bank have been major issuers of green bonds, mobilizing billions of dollars for renewable energy projects globally.

Green bond certification frameworks, such as those established by the Climate Bonds Initiative, ensure transparency and accountability, enhancing investor confidence. As the market for green bonds continues to grow, they play an increasingly important role in financing the renewable energy transition.

Blended Finance

Blended finance combines public and private capital to de-risk renewable energy investments and attract private sector participation. Public funds, such as grants, concessional loans, or guarantees, are used to absorb some of the risks associated with renewable energy projects, making them more appealing to private investors.

This mechanism is particularly effective in high-risk markets, such as developing nations or early-stage technologies. For example, blended finance can support off-grid solar projects in rural areas by reducing upfront costs and guaranteeing a minimum return for investors. Organizations like the GCF and the CIF frequently use blended finance models to catalyze private sector investment in renewable energy.

The collaborative nature of blended finance ensures that public funds are used strategically, leveraging significantly larger volumes of private capital. This approach not only accelerates renewable energy deployment but also promotes economic development in underserved regions.

Pay-as-You-Go Models

PAYG financing models enable households and businesses to access renewable energy technologies without significant upfront costs. Under this mechanism, users make small, incremental payments based on their energy consumption, typically using mobile payment systems. PAYG has been particularly successful in expanding access to solar home systems and microgrids in off-grid regions.

For example, companies like M-KOPA and Fenix International have used PAYG models to provide affordable solar solutions to millions of households in sub-Saharan Africa. These systems often include solar panels, batteries, and LED lights, allowing users to generate and store electricity for daily use.

The flexibility of PAYG models makes them an effective solution for low-income households, as payments can be tailored to align with users' financial capacity. Additionally, PAYG systems often include financing options that allow customers to eventually own the renewable energy systems outright, promoting long-term energy independence.

Crowdfunding

Crowdfunding platforms allow individuals and organizations to pool resources and collectively invest in renewable energy projects. This mechanism democratizes renewable energy financing, enabling smaller investors to participate in projects that were previously accessible only to large financial institutions or wealthy individuals.

Platforms like Mosaic and Abundance Investment have successfully funded renewable energy initiatives by connecting investors with developers. Investors can earn returns based on the performance of the projects, while developers gain access to capital without relying on traditional financial institutions.

Crowdfunding is particularly effective for community-led renewable energy projects, where local stakeholders can contribute to initiatives that directly benefit their communities. By fostering a sense of ownership and engagement, crowdfunding strengthens support for renewable energy at the grassroots level.

Energy-as-a-Service (EaaS)

The Energy-as-a-Service model shifts the financial burden of renewable energy adoption from end-users to service providers. Under this arrangement, a company installs, operates, and maintains renewable energy systems on behalf of the user, who pays for the energy consumed as a service. This eliminates the need for users to make large capital investments in renewable energy infrastructure.

For example, solar-as-a-service companies like Sunrun and SolarCity install rooftop solar systems at no upfront cost to homeowners. Instead, customers sign long-term agreements to purchase the electricity generated by the systems. This model lowers barriers to entry for residential and commercial users, making renewable energy more accessible.

EaaS is also gaining traction in the industrial and commercial sectors, where businesses can benefit from cost savings and predictable energy pricing without investing in on-site renewable energy systems. By outsourcing energy generation and management, companies can focus on their core operations while reducing their carbon footprint.

Chapter 7: Strengthening International Energy Partnerships

The global nature of the renewable energy transition demands robust international collaboration. Strengthening international energy partnerships is critical for addressing shared challenges, such as climate change, energy security, and equitable access to clean energy technologies. These partnerships enable countries to pool resources, share expertise, and align policies to accelerate the adoption of renewable energy worldwide.

This chapter explores the role of international cooperation in scaling up renewable energy deployment. It examines key areas for collaboration, including technology transfer, financing, capacity building, and policy harmonization. Additionally, it highlights the importance of fostering partnerships between governments, international organizations, private sector stakeholders, and research institutions to drive innovation and support energy transitions in both developed and developing nations.

By focusing on collaborative approaches, this chapter provides actionable insights for policymakers and stakeholders to enhance global energy partnerships. Strengthened cooperation not only advances renewable energy goals but also promotes economic development, fosters innovation, and ensures a more sustainable and equitable energy future for all.

Importance of Global Cooperation in Renewable Energy

Global cooperation is essential for accelerating the transition to renewable energy and addressing the challenges posed by climate change, energy security, and equitable access to clean energy. The renewable energy transition is not confined by borders; its benefits and impacts are inherently global. As such, fostering international collaboration allows countries to leverage shared resources, exchange knowledge, and align strategies to achieve common energy and climate goals. This chapter explores why global cooperation is crucial for the renewable energy transition and highlights the key areas where international efforts can make a significant impact.

Addressing Climate Change

Climate change is a global challenge that requires collective action to mitigate its effects and reduce greenhouse gas emissions. Renewable energy plays a central role in decarbonizing energy systems, but the scale of investment and deployment needed cannot be achieved by individual countries alone. Global cooperation enables the pooling of resources and expertise, ensuring that renewable energy technologies are developed and deployed at a scale sufficient to meet international climate targets, such as those outlined in the Paris Agreement.

For example, international initiatives like the International Solar Alliance (ISA) bring countries together to promote the adoption of solar energy technologies. By sharing best practices, providing technical assistance, and facilitating financing, such initiatives enhance global efforts to reduce emissions and promote renewable energy.

Sharing Technology and Knowledge

One of the most significant benefits of global cooperation is the ability to share technology and knowledge across borders. Many countries lack the technical expertise or access to advanced renewable energy technologies needed to drive their energy transitions. International collaboration can bridge this gap by facilitating technology transfer, training programs, and research partnerships.

For instance, developed countries with established renewable energy industries can share innovations in solar, wind, and energy storage technologies with developing nations. This not only accelerates the adoption of renewable energy in underserved regions but also helps create new markets for renewable energy manufacturers and developers. Programs such as the Clean Energy Ministerial (CEM) provide platforms for governments and private sector stakeholders to collaborate on advancing clean energy technologies globally.

Mobilizing Financial Resources

The financial resources required for the global renewable energy transition are immense. Developing nations, in particular, face significant challenges in accessing capital for renewable energy projects due to high perceived risks, limited credit availability, and underdeveloped financial markets. Global cooperation is critical in mobilizing the financial resources needed to overcome these barriers.

Multilateral development banks, international climate funds, and bilateral agreements play a crucial role in financing renewable energy projects in developing countries. Initiatives such as the GCF and the CIF provide concessional loans, grants, and guarantees to support renewable energy projects in high-risk markets. By leveraging public funds to attract private investment, these international efforts help ensure that renewable energy projects are financially viable and scalable.

Promoting Energy Security

Energy security is a concern for all nations, as disruptions in energy supply can have significant economic and social consequences. Renewable energy provides an opportunity to reduce dependence on fossil fuel imports and diversify energy sources, but international collaboration is necessary to realize its full potential. For instance, cross-border energy trade and interconnected power grids can enhance regional energy security by enabling countries to share renewable energy resources.

The European Union's Internal Energy Market is a prime example of how regional cooperation can improve energy security. By integrating national energy markets and fostering cross-border electricity trade, EU member states can optimize renewable energy generation and balance supply and demand across the region. Similar initiatives in other regions, such as Africa's Continental Power System Master Plan, demonstrate the importance of cooperation in strengthening energy security globally.

Ensuring Equitable Access

Global cooperation is also essential for ensuring that the benefits of renewable energy are distributed equitably. Many developing countries and marginalized communities still lack access to reliable and affordable energy. International collaboration can help address this disparity by providing technical assistance, financing, and capacity building to underserved regions.

Programs like the United Nations' Sustainable Energy for All (SEforALL) initiative aim to ensure universal access to modern energy services by fostering partnerships between governments, development agencies, and private sector stakeholders. By prioritizing energy access in international cooperation efforts, these programs contribute to poverty alleviation, improved health outcomes, and economic development in vulnerable regions.

Strengthening Policy Alignment

Harmonized policies and standards are vital for facilitating the global transition to renewable energy. Divergent regulatory frameworks and technical standards can create barriers to trade, investment, and technology deployment. Global cooperation allows countries to align policies and standards, making it easier to scale renewable energy projects and integrate technologies across borders.

For example, international agreements on carbon pricing, emissions reduction targets, and renewable energy incentives can create a level playing field for businesses and investors. Organizations like the IRENA play a key role in fostering policy dialogue and promoting harmonized approaches to renewable energy governance.

Multilateral Agreements and Initiatives for Renewable Energy

Multilateral agreements and initiatives play a critical role in driving global efforts toward renewable energy adoption. By fostering international collaboration, these frameworks provide a platform for countries to align their goals, share resources, and address common challenges. Multilateral efforts also enable the mobilization of significant financial and technical resources, ensuring that both developed and developing nations can participate in the renewable energy transition. This chapter examines the importance of multilateral agreements and initiatives, highlighting key examples and their impact on the global energy landscape.

The Role of Multilateral Agreements

Multilateral agreements set the stage for coordinated international action on renewable energy and climate change. These agreements establish shared objectives, commitments, and mechanisms for monitoring progress, creating a sense of accountability among signatories. By addressing transnational challenges, such as greenhouse gas emissions and energy security, these agreements ensure that no country is left behind in the global transition to renewable energy.

One of the most significant benefits of multilateral agreements is their ability to bring together diverse stakeholders, including governments, private sector entities, and civil society organizations. This inclusivity fosters innovation, facilitates knowledge sharing, and strengthens the collective capacity to address complex energy challenges.

Key Multilateral Agreements

The Paris Agreement (2015):

The Paris Agreement is a landmark global accord adopted by nearly 200 countries to combat climate change and accelerate the transition to clean energy. The agreement aims to limit global warming to well below 2°C above pre-industrial levels, with efforts to restrict it to 1.5°C. Each country commits to NDCs, outlining their plans for emissions reductions and renewable energy deployment.

The Paris Agreement has been instrumental in promoting renewable energy as a key strategy for achieving emissions reductions. By encouraging countries to set ambitious targets and report their progress, the agreement has created a global framework for accountability and cooperation. It has also spurred investments in renewable energy, with many countries integrating clean energy goals into their NDCs.

Sustainable Development Goals (SDGs):

Adopted by the United Nations in 2015, the SDGs include Goal 7: Affordable and Clean Energy, which aims to ensure universal access to modern energy services, increase the share of renewable energy in the global energy mix, and improve energy efficiency. This goal aligns closely with other SDGs, such as those related to climate action, poverty reduction, and economic growth.

The SDGs provide a comprehensive framework for integrating renewable energy into broader development objectives. Through partnerships between governments, international organizations, and private sector actors, the SDGs have mobilized resources and attention toward expanding renewable energy access, particularly in underserved regions.

International Renewable Energy Agency:

IRENA is an intergovernmental organization dedicated to promoting the widespread adoption and sustainable use of renewable energy. Established in 2009, IRENA provides a platform for 167 member states to collaborate on renewable energy policies, technology development, and capacity building.

IRENA's initiatives include the Global Energy Transformation report, which outlines pathways for scaling up renewable energy to meet global climate goals, and the Clean Energy Corridor, which supports regional renewable energy integration in Africa, Asia, and Latin America. By facilitating dialogue and technical assistance, IRENA has become a key player in advancing renewable energy globally.

Regional Initiatives

European Green Deal:

The European Union's Green Deal is a comprehensive policy framework aimed at achieving net-zero greenhouse gas emissions by 2050. Renewable energy is a cornerstone of this strategy, with targets to increase the share of renewables in the EU energy mix to at least 32% by 2030. The Green Deal also emphasizes cross-border energy cooperation, infrastructure development, and innovation.

Through initiatives such as the Renewable Energy Directive and the Connecting Europe Facility, the EU supports renewable energy projects across member states, enhancing regional energy security and sustainability.

African Renewable Energy Initiative (AREI):

AREI is a continental initiative led by African countries to accelerate the deployment of renewable energy in Africa. Launched in 2015, the initiative aims to install at least 300 gigawatts (GW) of renewable energy capacity by 2030. AREI focuses on promoting decentralized energy systems, addressing energy access gaps, and mobilizing international support for renewable energy projects.

By aligning national and regional efforts, AREI has attracted significant funding from international donors and development banks, facilitating the implementation of renewable energy projects in remote and underserved areas.

Financial Mechanisms in Multilateral Initiatives

Multilateral agreements and initiatives often include financial mechanisms to support renewable energy projects, particularly in developing countries. These mechanisms reduce financial barriers, de-risk investments, and catalyze private sector participation.

Green Climate Fund:

The GCF is a key financial instrument under the Paris Agreement, providing grants, loans, and guarantees to support climate adaptation and mitigation projects. Renewable energy is a primary focus of the GCF, which has financed projects ranging from solar power installations in Africa to wind energy development in Asia.

Climate Investment Funds:

CIF channels resources to developing countries to support renewable energy and climate resilience. Its programs, such as the Scaling Up Renewable Energy Program (SREP) and the Clean Technology Fund (CTF), provide concessional finance to accelerate renewable energy deployment and innovation.

Challenges and Opportunities

While multilateral agreements and initiatives have made significant contributions to the renewable energy transition, challenges remain. These include ensuring equitable access to resources, addressing geopolitical tensions, and maintaining accountability among participating countries. Additionally, translating high-level commitments into tangible projects on the ground requires strong national policies and institutional capacity.

However, the opportunities for multilateral collaboration are vast. By fostering innovation, leveraging financial resources, and promoting knowledge sharing, multilateral initiatives can accelerate progress toward a sustainable energy future. Strengthening these efforts and ensuring inclusive participation will be critical to achieving global renewable energy goals.

Knowledge and Technology Sharing in Renewable Energy

Knowledge and technology sharing are critical components of the global renewable energy transition. As countries strive to meet ambitious energy and climate goals, the exchange of expertise, data, and innovations can help accelerate progress, reduce costs, and ensure that all regions have access to clean energy solutions. By fostering collaboration between governments, businesses, research institutions, and international organizations, knowledge and technology sharing enables the efficient deployment of renewable energy technologies and addresses disparities in technical capacity.

The Role of Knowledge Sharing

Knowledge sharing involves the exchange of information, best practices, and lessons learned from renewable energy projects and policies. This process helps countries and organizations avoid common pitfalls, optimize their approaches, and adapt successful strategies to their unique contexts.

For example, countries with advanced renewable energy sectors can share their experiences in integrating solar and wind power into national grids, managing energy storage systems, or implementing regulatory frameworks. Similarly, developing countries can share insights on deploying decentralized energy systems in off-grid communities, providing valuable perspectives on localized challenges and solutions.

Knowledge sharing platforms, such as the IRENA and the Clean Energy Ministerial (CEM), facilitate this exchange by providing forums for dialogue, publishing case studies, and organizing training workshops. These platforms enable stakeholders to learn from one another and adopt proven strategies for renewable energy deployment.

Technology Transfer

Technology transfer refers to the process of sharing renewable energy technologies, including their design, production, and operational know-how, from one country or organization to another. This is particularly important for developing nations that may lack the resources or expertise to develop advanced technologies independently.

Mechanisms for Technology Transfer:

• **Public-Private Partnerships:** Governments can collaborate with private companies to transfer renewable energy technologies to underserved regions. For instance, a company specializing in solar photovoltaic systems might establish manufacturing facilities in a developing country, providing both technology and job opportunities.

• **International Agreements:** Multilateral agreements often include provisions for technology transfer. For example, the Paris Agreement emphasizes the need for developed countries to support developing nations through technology sharing and capacity building.

• **Bilateral Partnerships:** Countries can form direct agreements to share technologies. For instance, a country with expertise in wind energy might assist another in developing its own wind power infrastructure.

Examples of Successful Technology Transfer:

• **China's Solar Industry:** China's rise as a global leader in solar energy was supported by technology transfer from countries like Germany and the United States. This knowledge exchange helped China scale up its manufacturing capacity and reduce the cost of solar panels worldwide.

• **Off-Grid Solar in Africa:** International initiatives, such as Power Africa, have facilitated the transfer of solar technologies to rural areas across the continent, enabling millions to access electricity for the first time.

Capacity Building

Knowledge and technology sharing go hand in hand with capacity building, which involves training individuals, institutions, and governments to develop and manage renewable energy systems. Capacity building ensures that countries have the human resources and institutional frameworks needed to implement and sustain renewable energy initiatives.

Key Areas for Capacity Building:

• **Technical Training:** Providing hands-on training for engineers, technicians, and project managers ensures that renewable energy systems are installed, operated, and maintained effectively.

• **Policy Development:** Training policymakers on renewable energy regulations, incentives, and market mechanisms helps create supportive environments for clean energy deployment.

• **R&D:** Building research capacity enables countries to adapt renewable energy technologies to local conditions and innovate new solutions.

International organizations, such as the United Nations Development Programme (UNDP), frequently conduct capacity-building programs in developing countries. These programs focus on developing technical skills, fostering innovation, and strengthening institutions.

Addressing Barriers to Knowledge and Technology Sharing

Despite its importance, knowledge and technology sharing faces several barriers, including intellectual property restrictions, geopolitical tensions, and limited financial resources. Overcoming these challenges requires coordinated efforts and supportive policies.

Solutions to Enhance Sharing:

• **Open Access Initiatives:** Encouraging open access to research, data, and technology designs can reduce barriers to knowledge sharing. For instance, open-source platforms for renewable energy software allow developers worldwide to access and improve upon existing tools.

• **Financial Support:** Funding from international organizations and development banks can help cover the costs of technology transfer and capacity-building initiatives.

• **Policy Coordination:** Harmonizing intellectual property regulations and fostering international cooperation can ease tensions and promote the exchange of knowledge and technology.

The Impact of Knowledge and Technology Sharing

The benefits of knowledge and technology sharing extend beyond renewable energy deployment. By fostering collaboration and building trust among nations, these efforts contribute to global economic development, job creation, and environmental sustainability. Furthermore, sharing innovations can lead to cost reductions and efficiency improvements, making renewable energy more accessible to all.

Chapter 8: Overcoming Challenges in Collaboration

While collaboration is critical to advancing renewable energy on a global scale, it is not without its challenges. Differences in priorities, resource availability, technological capabilities, and policy frameworks can create barriers to effective cooperation. Geopolitical tensions, competition over resources, and mismatched objectives among stakeholders further complicate efforts to build cohesive partnerships. Addressing these obstacles is essential to unlocking the full potential of international collaboration and ensuring that the renewable energy transition benefits all.

This chapter delves into the common challenges faced in collaborative efforts to promote renewable energy and explores strategies to overcome them. It examines issues such as regulatory and cultural disparities, financial constraints, and the complexities of technology transfer. By identifying practical solutions, such as aligning policies, fostering trust, and enhancing communication, this chapter provides a roadmap for strengthening partnerships among governments, private sectors, and international organizations.

Overcoming these challenges is not only key to accelerating the renewable energy transition but also to fostering innovation, improving global energy equity, and ensuring a sustainable future for all.

Addressing Geopolitical Tensions in Renewable Energy Collaboration

Geopolitical tensions pose significant challenges to the global transition to renewable energy. As countries strive to secure energy resources, establish market dominance, and achieve national energy independence, conflicting interests can undermine international collaboration. These tensions can hinder the exchange of knowledge, technology, and financial resources necessary for renewable energy deployment. Addressing geopolitical barriers is essential for fostering cooperation, ensuring equitable access to clean energy, and advancing shared climate goals.

Energy Resource Competition

The competition for critical materials required in renewable energy technologies is a key driver of geopolitical tensions. Elements such as lithium, cobalt, and rare earth metals are essential for manufacturing batteries, solar panels, and wind turbines. However, the extraction and production of these resources are concentrated in a few countries, creating vulnerabilities in global supply chains and intensifying geopolitical rivalries.

For instance, China's dominance in rare earth metal production has raised concerns among other nations about supply security and market control. Similarly, the Democratic Republic of Congo, which supplies over 70% of the world's cobalt, faces challenges related to governance and resource management, leading to concerns about stability and fair trade practices.

To address these tensions, countries can diversify their supply chains by investing in domestic resource development, recycling programs, and alternative materials. International agreements on resource management and trade can also promote transparency, reduce monopolistic practices, and ensure fair access to critical materials.

Technology and Intellectual Property Disputes

Technological advancements in renewable energy are critical for achieving global energy transitions, but intellectual property (IP) disputes can hinder knowledge sharing and technology transfer. Countries and companies may be reluctant to share innovations due to concerns about losing competitive advantages or facing unauthorized use of proprietary technologies.

To mitigate these issues, international frameworks can be established to balance the protection of IP rights with the need for technology dissemination. For example, licensing agreements and technology partnerships can enable the controlled sharing of renewable energy innovations while ensuring fair compensation for developers. Multilateral organizations, such as the World Intellectual Property Organization (WIPO), can facilitate negotiations and establish guidelines to foster trust among stakeholders.

Trade Barriers and Tariffs

Trade restrictions, including tariffs on renewable energy technologies, can escalate geopolitical tensions and slow the deployment of clean energy systems. For instance, disputes over solar panel imports between major economies, such as the United States and China, have disrupted global supply chains and increased costs for developers.

Reducing trade barriers is essential for promoting international cooperation and facilitating the widespread adoption of renewable energy. Policymakers can negotiate trade agreements that prioritize clean energy technologies, eliminate tariffs, and standardize product regulations. Regional trade blocs, such as the European Union, provide successful examples of harmonized trade policies that support renewable energy markets.

Geopolitical Tensions in Energy Infrastructure

Disputes over cross-border energy infrastructure, such as transmission lines and pipelines, can create significant geopolitical challenges. While regional energy grids and renewable energy trade agreements offer opportunities for collaboration, they also require extensive coordination and mutual trust among participating countries.

For example, the development of regional power grids in Africa and Asia has faced delays due to disagreements over funding, governance, and resource allocation. Similarly, the expansion of renewable energy projects in disputed territories, such as offshore wind farms in contested maritime zones, can exacerbate geopolitical tensions.

To address these challenges, countries can establish multilateral agreements that outline shared responsibilities, benefits, and conflict resolution mechanisms. Institutions such as the IRENA and regional energy organizations can act as neutral mediators, facilitating dialogue and ensuring transparency in cross-border energy initiatives.

Addressing Energy Transition Inequities

The unequal distribution of resources and capabilities for renewable energy adoption contributes to geopolitical tensions, particularly between developed and developing nations. Wealthier countries often have greater access to capital, technology, and expertise, while developing nations struggle to secure the resources needed for their energy transitions. This disparity can lead to mistrust and reluctance to engage in collaborative efforts.

To address these inequities, international funding mechanisms, such as the GCF and the CIF, play a crucial role in supporting renewable energy projects in developing countries. Additionally, developed nations can provide financial and technical assistance, capacity building, and technology transfer to ensure that all countries benefit from the renewable energy transition.

Building Trust and Fostering Dialogue

Building trust and fostering open dialogue are essential for resolving geopolitical tensions and promoting cooperation in renewable energy. Regular communication and transparent decision-making processes can reduce misunderstandings and ensure that all stakeholders feel included in collaborative efforts.

Multilateral organizations, such as the United Nations Framework Convention on Climate Change (UNFCCC), provide platforms for dialogue and negotiation, allowing countries to address their concerns and align their objectives. Similarly, regional forums and bilateral partnerships can facilitate trust-building and conflict resolution.

Equitable Participation of Developing Nations in Renewable Energy Transition

The equitable participation of developing nations in the global renewable energy transition is critical for achieving sustainable and inclusive growth. While many developing countries possess abundant renewable energy resources, such as solar, wind, and hydropower, they often face significant barriers to accessing the financial, technological, and institutional support needed to harness these resources. Ensuring that developing nations can participate equitably in the renewable energy revolution not only addresses global energy disparities but also promotes economic development, enhances energy security, and accelerates climate action.

Challenges Faced by Developing Nations

Developing nations encounter unique challenges that hinder their ability to participate equitably in the renewable energy transition. These challenges often stem from financial constraints, limited technological capacity, and underdeveloped infrastructure.

Financial Barriers:

High upfront costs for renewable energy projects, combined with limited access to affordable credit, pose significant hurdles for developing countries. Many governments in these nations struggle to allocate resources for renewable energy due to competing priorities such as healthcare, education, and basic infrastructure. Furthermore, private investors often perceive renewable energy projects in developing nations as high-risk due to political instability, regulatory uncertainties, and currency fluctuations.

Technological Gaps:

While renewable energy technologies have become more affordable in recent years, many developing countries lack the expertise and technical capacity needed to deploy and maintain these systems. This gap limits their ability to integrate renewable energy into existing energy systems and hinders innovation in localized solutions.

Infrastructure Deficits:

Underdeveloped infrastructure, such as transmission grids, storage systems, and transportation networks, poses a significant challenge to renewable energy deployment. Rural and remote areas, where renewable energy can have the greatest impact, often lack the infrastructure needed to support large-scale projects or decentralized energy systems.

Importance of Equitable Participation

Equitable participation in renewable energy transitions is essential for addressing global energy inequality and achieving sustainable development. Ensuring that developing nations can access the resources and support needed for their energy transitions yields multiple benefits.

Climate Action:

Developing nations are often disproportionately affected by the impacts of climate change, including extreme weather events, rising sea levels, and resource scarcity. Renewable energy offers a pathway to reduce greenhouse gas emissions while increasing resilience to climate-related challenges.

Economic Development:

Investing in renewable energy can stimulate economic growth by creating jobs, attracting investments, and diversifying economies. For example, building solar farms or wind turbines creates employment opportunities across the value chain, from construction and maintenance to manufacturing and distribution.

Energy Access and Security:

Renewable energy can provide affordable and reliable electricity to underserved communities, particularly in rural and remote areas. Expanding access to clean energy enhances quality of life, supports education and healthcare, and reduces reliance on imported fossil fuels.

Strategies to Ensure Equitable Participation

Promoting equitable participation of developing nations in the renewable energy transition requires targeted strategies and coordinated efforts by governments, international organizations, and private sector stakeholders.

Financial Support:

International funding mechanisms, such as the GCF and the CIF, play a critical role in mobilizing resources for renewable energy projects in developing nations. These funds provide grants, concessional loans, and guarantees that reduce financial barriers and attract private sector investment.

Blended finance models, which combine public and private funding, are another effective tool for supporting renewable energy projects in high-risk markets. By de-risking investments, blended finance encourages greater participation from private investors and accelerates project implementation.

Technology Transfer and Capacity Building:

Technology transfer is essential for bridging the technological gap in developing nations. International partnerships can facilitate the sharing of renewable energy technologies and expertise, enabling countries to deploy and adapt solutions to their unique contexts. For example, developed countries can provide technical assistance for solar panel installation, wind farm development, or energy storage integration.

Capacity building complements technology transfer by equipping individuals, institutions, and governments with the skills and knowledge needed to manage renewable energy systems. Training programs for engineers, policymakers, and community leaders ensure that renewable energy projects are implemented and sustained effectively.

Policy and Regulatory Support:

Establishing supportive policy and regulatory frameworks is critical for attracting investment and promoting renewable energy in developing nations. Governments can implement policies such as feed-in tariffs, tax incentives, and renewable energy quotas to create a favorable environment for clean energy projects. Simplifying permitting processes and ensuring transparent governance further enhance investor confidence.

International organizations, such as the IRENA, provide guidance and technical assistance to help developing nations design and implement effective energy policies.

Decentralized Energy Solutions:

Decentralized renewable energy systems, such as mini-grids and standalone solar home systems, offer an effective solution for expanding energy access in rural and remote areas. These systems are often more cost-effective and faster to deploy than traditional grid extensions. Programs like the United Nations' Sustainable Energy for All (SEforALL) initiative support the development of decentralized energy solutions, ensuring that no community is left behind in the energy transition.

The Role of International Collaboration

International collaboration is essential for ensuring the equitable participation of developing nations in the renewable energy transition. Multilateral agreements, such as the Paris Agreement, emphasize the need for developed countries to support developing nations through financial assistance, technology sharing, and capacity building. Collaborative initiatives, such as Power Africa and the African Renewable Energy Initiative (AREI), demonstrate the potential of partnerships to accelerate renewable energy deployment in underserved regions.

Additionally, fostering South-South cooperation—collaboration among developing nations—can enhance knowledge exchange and resource sharing. Countries with similar challenges and contexts can work together to develop scalable and sustainable renewable energy solutions.

Frameworks for Successful Collaboration in Renewable Energy

Effective collaboration is essential for advancing the renewable energy transition on a global scale. The complex nature of this transition requires input from multiple stakeholders, including governments, private sector entities, research institutions, and international organizations. Collaborative frameworks provide the structure and guidelines necessary to coordinate these efforts, align objectives, and ensure accountability. By fostering trust, transparency, and efficiency, well-designed frameworks enable stakeholders to overcome barriers, share resources, and achieve common energy goals.

Defining Collaborative Frameworks

Collaborative frameworks are structured systems or agreements that outline the roles, responsibilities, and processes for cooperation among stakeholders. These frameworks serve as blueprints for successful partnerships, addressing critical aspects such as decision-making, resource allocation, conflict resolution, and performance evaluation.

In the context of renewable energy, collaborative frameworks can take various forms, including multilateral agreements, PPPs, and regional energy initiatives. Regardless of their form, effective frameworks share common characteristics, such as clear objectives, transparent governance, and inclusive participation.

Key Components of Effective Frameworks

1. Clear Objectives and Shared Goals:

Successful collaboration begins with a clear understanding of the objectives and desired outcomes. Stakeholders must align their goals, such as reducing greenhouse gas emissions, increasing renewable energy capacity, or improving energy access. Shared objectives foster unity and provide a common direction for collaborative efforts.

2. Inclusive Stakeholder Engagement:

Collaboration should involve a diverse range of stakeholders, including governments, private companies, local communities, and non-governmental organizations (NGOs). Inclusive engagement ensures that all perspectives are considered, leading to more equitable and effective outcomes. For example, involving local communities in renewable energy projects can enhance social acceptance and address region-specific challenges.

3. Transparent Governance and Accountability:

Transparency in decision-making and resource allocation is critical for building trust among stakeholders. Collaborative frameworks should establish clear governance structures, with defined roles and responsibilities for each participant. Regular reporting, monitoring, and evaluation mechanisms help ensure accountability and measure progress toward agreed goals.

4. Flexible and Adaptive Structures:

Renewable energy projects often face dynamic challenges, such as changing market conditions, technological advancements, and evolving regulatory environments. Collaborative frameworks must be flexible enough to adapt to these changes without compromising their core objectives. For instance, agreements should allow for revisions to timelines, budgets, or project designs as needed.

5. Conflict Resolution Mechanisms:

Disputes among stakeholders can hinder collaboration and delay progress. Effective frameworks include mechanisms for resolving conflicts in a fair and timely manner. Mediation, arbitration, or the involvement of neutral third parties can help address disagreements and maintain the integrity of the partnership.

Examples of Collaborative Frameworks

Multilateral Agreements:

Multilateral frameworks, such as the Paris Agreement, provide a global structure for renewable energy collaboration. By committing to Nationally Determined Contributions (NDCs), countries align their renewable energy targets with international climate goals. The agreement also fosters knowledge sharing and financial support through mechanisms like the Green Climate Fund.

Public-Private Partnerships:

PPPs are a common collaborative framework for renewable energy projects, particularly in infrastructure development. For example, governments may partner with private companies to finance, build, and operate solar farms or wind parks. The public sector provides regulatory support and guarantees, while the private sector contributes expertise and capital.

Regional Energy Initiatives:

Regional frameworks, such as the European Union's Internal Energy Market, enable cross-border collaboration on renewable energy. These initiatives facilitate the integration of national energy systems, promote resource sharing, and enhance energy security across member states.

Benefits of Collaborative Frameworks

Collaborative frameworks offer numerous benefits, including:

• **Resource Efficiency:** By pooling financial, technical, and human resources, frameworks reduce duplication of efforts and optimize the use of available assets.

• **Knowledge Sharing:** Structured collaboration enables stakeholders to exchange expertise, best practices, and innovations, accelerating renewable energy deployment.

• **Risk Mitigation:** Shared responsibilities and risk-sharing mechanisms make renewable energy projects more attractive to investors and reduce financial uncertainties.

• **Enhanced Scalability:** Frameworks provide the structure needed to scale successful projects and replicate them in other regions or contexts.

Challenges and Solutions

Despite their advantages, collaborative frameworks face challenges such as misaligned priorities, power imbalances, and limited capacity among stakeholders. To address these issues, stakeholders should prioritize open communication, invest in capacity building, and establish mechanisms to ensure equitable participation. Additionally, fostering a culture of mutual respect and shared accountability can strengthen partnerships and enhance long-term success.

Chapter 9: Modernizing Energy Infrastructure

Modernizing energy infrastructure is a cornerstone of the renewable energy transition. As the world shifts away from fossil fuels to cleaner energy sources, existing energy systems must be upgraded to accommodate new technologies and evolving demands. Renewable energy infrastructure, including smart grids, energy storage systems, and decentralized networks, requires innovation and investment to ensure reliability, efficiency, and scalability.

This chapter explores the critical need for infrastructure modernization to support the integration of renewable energy. It examines key challenges, such as aging grid systems, variability in renewable energy generation, and the need for flexible energy storage solutions. Additionally, the chapter highlights strategies for upgrading transmission and distribution networks, enhancing grid resilience, and fostering innovation in energy system design.

By addressing these issues, stakeholders can create a robust and adaptive infrastructure capable of meeting global energy demands while promoting sustainability and resilience. This chapter provides actionable insights for policymakers, energy companies, and other stakeholders to ensure that energy infrastructure modernization remains a priority in the renewable energy transition.

Upgrading Grid Infrastructure for Renewable Energy Integration

The modernization of grid infrastructure is a critical requirement for the successful integration of renewable energy into global energy systems. Traditional grid designs, built to handle centralized, fossil fuel-based generation, face significant challenges in accommodating the decentralized, variable nature of renewable energy sources such as solar and wind. Upgrading grid infrastructure ensures that electricity generated from renewables can be transmitted, distributed, and managed efficiently, reliably, and sustainably. This section explores the need for grid upgrades, key components of modernization, and strategies to overcome associated challenges.

The Need for Grid Modernization

The growing adoption of renewable energy has fundamentally changed the way electricity is generated, distributed, and consumed. Unlike fossil fuel plants, which provide consistent output, renewable energy sources are intermittent, as their generation depends on weather conditions. For example, solar panels produce electricity during daylight hours, while wind turbines generate power only when the wind blows. This variability requires grid infrastructure to become more flexible and adaptive.

Additionally, the decentralization of energy systems, driven by rooftop solar installations, community microgrids, and distributed energy resources (DERs), places new demands on grid infrastructure. Traditional grids designed for one-way electricity flows—from large power plants to consumers—must now manage two-way flows, where electricity can be generated, stored, and consumed at various points within the system.

Key Components of Grid Upgrades

1. Transmission and Distribution Networks:

Modernizing transmission and distribution networks is essential to accommodate the increased generation of renewable energy, often located in remote areas. For instance, wind farms are typically situated in rural regions or offshore, far from population centers. Expanding and upgrading transmission lines ensures that electricity can be transported efficiently from generation sites to demand centers.

Upgrades to distribution networks are equally important, particularly in urban areas with high penetration of rooftop solar and electric vehicles (EVs). Strengthening local grids ensures that they can handle increased loads and bidirectional energy flows.

2. Energy Storage Integration:

Energy storage systems, such as batteries, play a vital role in stabilizing grids by storing excess electricity generated during periods of high renewable output and releasing it during periods of low generation. Integrating large-scale storage into grid infrastructure helps balance supply and demand, reducing the need for fossil fuel-based backup power.

3. Smart Grid Technology:

Smart grids leverage advanced technologies, such as sensors, automation, and real-time data analytics, to improve grid efficiency and reliability. These systems enable dynamic adjustments to electricity flows, better forecasting of renewable energy generation, and faster responses to disruptions. For example, smart grids can optimize the use of distributed energy resources, prioritize renewable energy dispatch, and detect faults in the system before they lead to outages.

4. Grid Resilience Enhancements:

As climate change increases the frequency of extreme weather events, grid resilience has become a priority. Modernized grids are designed to withstand natural disasters, reduce downtime, and recover quickly from disruptions. Resilience measures include undergrounding power lines, reinforcing critical infrastructure, and deploying microgrids in vulnerable areas.

Challenges in Upgrading Grid Infrastructure

While grid modernization is essential, it comes with significant challenges that must be addressed to ensure successful implementation.

1. High Costs:

Upgrading grid infrastructure requires substantial investment, particularly for large-scale transmission projects and the deployment of advanced technologies. Financing these upgrades can be challenging for governments and utilities, particularly in developing countries.

2. Regulatory Barriers:

Inconsistent or outdated regulations can hinder grid modernization efforts. For instance, policies that fail to support renewable energy integration or distributed energy resources may delay necessary upgrades.

3. Public Opposition:

Expanding transmission lines and other grid infrastructure can face resistance from local communities due to environmental concerns or land use conflicts. Stakeholder engagement and transparent planning processes are essential to address these concerns.

4. Technological Integration:

The integration of diverse technologies, such as energy storage and smart grid systems, requires careful planning and coordination. Ensuring compatibility and interoperability between different components is a complex but critical aspect of grid upgrades.

Strategies for Successful Grid Modernization

1. Public and Private Investment:

Governments and utilities must prioritize funding for grid upgrades, leveraging public-private partnerships to mobilize additional resources. Mechanisms such as green bonds and infrastructure funds can help finance large-scale projects.

2. Regulatory Reform:

Policymakers should establish clear and supportive regulations that promote renewable energy integration and incentivize investments in grid modernization. This includes updating interconnection standards, enabling net metering, and encouraging innovation in energy storage.

3. Stakeholder Collaboration:

Engaging local communities, businesses, and environmental groups in the planning process can build consensus and reduce opposition to grid projects. Collaborative approaches ensure that infrastructure upgrades meet the needs of all stakeholders.

4. Innovation and Research:

Continued investment in R&D is essential to advance grid technologies and improve their cost-effectiveness. Innovations such as high-voltage direct current (HVDC) transmission and advanced grid management software hold great potential for modernizing energy systems.

The Role of Energy Storage in Renewable Energy Integration

Energy storage plays a pivotal role in the global transition to renewable energy, addressing critical challenges such as variability, grid stability, and energy access. Renewable energy sources like solar and wind are inherently intermittent, producing electricity only when the sun shines or the wind blows. Energy storage systems bridge this gap by storing surplus electricity during periods of high generation and releasing it during times of low production or high demand. This capability ensures a reliable and stable energy supply, enabling greater integration of renewables into the energy system.

Addressing Renewable Energy Variability

One of the most significant challenges of renewable energy integration is its variability. Solar panels generate electricity during the day, while wind turbines depend on wind conditions that can fluctuate hourly or seasonally. This intermittency can lead to mismatches between electricity supply and demand, particularly in systems with high renewable energy penetration.

Energy storage provides a solution by decoupling electricity generation from consumption. For example:

• **Day-Night Shifts:** Batteries can store solar energy generated during the day for use at night when demand often peaks.

• **Seasonal Variability:** In regions where wind production is higher during certain seasons, energy storage can capture excess energy for use in months with lower output.

This capability significantly enhances the reliability of renewable energy systems, reducing dependence on fossil fuel-based backup power and contributing to the decarbonization of the energy sector.

Enhancing Grid Stability

Energy storage systems are critical for maintaining grid stability as renewable energy sources become a larger share of the electricity mix. Traditional grids are designed to handle predictable energy flows from centralized fossil fuel plants. In contrast, renewable energy introduces variability that can disrupt grid operations, causing frequency imbalances, voltage fluctuations, and even blackouts.

Energy storage addresses these challenges by providing several grid-stabilizing services:

• **Frequency Regulation:** By rapidly charging or discharging electricity, storage systems help maintain the balance between supply and demand, stabilizing grid frequency.

• **Voltage Support:** Storage systems can manage voltage levels, ensuring consistent power delivery across the grid.

• **Black Start Capability:** In the event of a grid outage, energy storage systems can supply the initial power needed to restart power plants and restore grid operations.

These capabilities make energy storage a vital component of modern grid infrastructure, enabling higher levels of renewable energy integration without compromising system reliability.

Supporting Decentralized Energy Systems

The rise of decentralized energy systems, such as rooftop solar panels, community microgrids, and DERs, has transformed the traditional energy landscape. Energy storage is a key enabler of this transition, allowing decentralized systems to operate independently or in conjunction with the main grid.

Key Benefits for Decentralized Systems:

• **Energy Independence:** Homeowners and communities with storage systems can store surplus energy generated on-site and use it during outages or periods of high demand.

• **Load Shifting:** Storage systems enable users to store electricity during off-peak hours when prices are lower and use it during peak hours, reducing energy costs.

• **Microgrid Resilience:** In remote or disaster-prone areas, energy storage enhances the reliability of microgrids, ensuring continuous power supply during grid outages.

By empowering individuals and communities, energy storage supports energy equity and resilience while reducing reliance on centralized fossil fuel generation.

Facilitating Electric Vehicle Integration

The growing adoption of EVs adds another dimension to the role of energy storage. EVs are essentially mobile storage units that can interact with the grid through V2G technology. This integration provides a twofold benefit:

• **Grid Support:** EV batteries can discharge electricity back to the grid during peak demand, reducing strain on the system.

• **Renewable Energy Utilization:** Charging EVs during periods of high renewable energy production optimizes the use of clean energy and reduces curtailment.

The dual role of EVs as energy consumers and providers underscores the importance of storage in managing the transition to sustainable transportation systems.

Enabling Energy Access in Remote Areas

In regions with limited or no access to centralized electricity grids, energy storage systems play a transformative role in enabling renewable energy adoption. Remote and rural areas often rely on diesel generators for power, which are costly and environmentally harmful. Energy storage, combined with renewable energy systems, provides a cleaner and more sustainable alternative.

Applications in Remote Areas:

• **Off-Grid Solutions:** Solar panels paired with batteries provide reliable electricity for lighting, refrigeration, and communication in off-grid communities.

• **Mini-Grids:** Storage systems enable mini-grids to manage electricity supply and demand, reducing dependence on external energy sources.

• **Disaster Recovery:** In disaster-prone regions, portable storage systems ensure critical infrastructure, such as hospitals and emergency shelters, remains powered during crises.

These applications demonstrate the potential of energy storage to bridge the energy access gap and promote sustainable development.

Types of Energy Storage Technologies

Several energy storage technologies support renewable energy integration, each with unique characteristics and applications:

• **Lithium-Ion Batteries:** The most widely used storage technology, lithium-ion batteries offer high energy density, efficiency, and scalability. They are ideal for residential systems, grid-scale projects, and electric vehicles.

• **Flow Batteries:** These systems store energy in liquid electrolytes, offering long-duration storage and scalability for grid applications.

• **Pumped Hydro Storage:** Using excess electricity to pump water to higher elevations, this technology stores energy as gravitational potential energy. It is the largest form of grid-scale storage but requires specific geographic conditions.

• **Thermal Energy Storage:** Storing energy in the form of heat or cold, this technology supports applications such as concentrated solar power (CSP) plants and industrial processes.

The continued advancement of these technologies will play a crucial role in expanding the capabilities of energy storage systems.

Overcoming Challenges in Energy Storage

Despite its critical role, energy storage faces several challenges that must be addressed to unlock its full potential:

• **High Costs:** While prices for storage technologies, particularly lithium-ion batteries, have declined significantly, upfront costs remain a barrier for widespread adoption. Incentives and subsidies can help make storage systems more affordable.

• **Environmental Impact:** Mining and processing materials for batteries, such as lithium and cobalt, raise environmental and ethical concerns. Developing recycling programs and alternative materials can mitigate these issues.

• **Policy and Regulatory Gaps:** The lack of supportive policies and clear regulatory frameworks hinders the integration of energy storage into grid systems. Policymakers must prioritize energy storage in their renewable energy strategies.

Addressing these challenges requires coordinated efforts from governments, industries, and research institutions.

Challenges of Intermittency in Renewable Energy

The intermittency of renewable energy sources such as solar and wind presents significant challenges to their integration into energy systems. Unlike fossil fuel-based power plants, which can produce electricity consistently, renewable energy generation depends on environmental conditions. Solar panels generate electricity only when the sun is shining, and wind turbines produce power only when there is sufficient wind. This variability in supply can lead to mismatches with demand, grid instability, and the need for backup systems. Addressing these challenges is critical to maximizing the potential of renewable energy while maintaining reliable and efficient energy systems.

Variability in Energy Supply

Intermittency is an inherent characteristic of solar and wind energy due to their reliance on natural weather patterns. This variability occurs on multiple timescales:

• **Daily Fluctuations:** Solar power generation peaks during the day and drops to zero at night, while wind speeds can vary within hours.

• **Seasonal Variations:** Solar and wind resources fluctuate across seasons, with higher solar output in summer and wind generation often peaking in winter in many regions.

These fluctuations can create challenges for matching energy supply with demand, particularly in systems with high renewable energy penetration. For example, electricity demand often peaks in the evening when solar generation is unavailable, leading to potential shortfalls.

Grid Stability Concerns

The intermittent nature of renewables poses risks to grid stability, as energy systems require a continuous balance between supply and demand to maintain proper frequency and voltage levels. Without this balance, the grid can experience disruptions, including blackouts or equipment failures.

Key Grid Stability Challenges:

• **Frequency Regulation:** Rapid changes in renewable energy output can cause frequency imbalances in the grid, requiring immediate corrective actions.

• **Voltage Fluctuations:** Variability in power generation can lead to inconsistent voltage levels, affecting the performance of electrical equipment.

• **Curtailment:** In some cases, excess renewable energy generation exceeds grid capacity, leading to the curtailment of energy that could otherwise be used.

These challenges necessitate advanced grid management strategies and technologies to ensure stable and reliable electricity delivery.

Dependence on Backup Systems

To address the intermittency of renewables, energy systems often rely on backup power sources, such as fossil fuel plants or hydropower, to fill gaps in supply. While these backup systems provide essential support, they can undermine the environmental benefits of renewable energy by contributing to greenhouse gas emissions.

Challenges of Backup Systems:

• **Cost:** Maintaining backup power capacity increases the overall cost of energy systems, as idle plants must be kept operational to meet sudden demand.

- **Environmental Impact:** Fossil fuel-based backup systems reduce the overall emissions reduction potential of renewable energy integration.

- **Inefficiency:** Ramping up and down conventional power plants to balance renewable variability can lead to inefficiencies and higher operational costs.

Developing low-carbon alternatives to backup systems, such as energy storage, is critical for minimizing these drawbacks.

Forecasting and Planning Limitations

Accurately predicting renewable energy output is essential for effective grid management, but forecasting remains a challenge due to the complex nature of weather patterns. While advancements in meteorology and data analytics have improved forecasting accuracy, unexpected weather events can still disrupt energy supply planning.

Limitations of Forecasting:

- **Short-Term Variability:** Sudden changes in weather conditions, such as cloud cover or wind gusts, can significantly impact renewable energy output.

- **Regional Differences:** Variability in renewable resources across different geographic regions complicates system-wide energy planning.

Improving forecasting capabilities and integrating them into grid management systems is essential for mitigating the impacts of intermittency.

Addressing Demand-Supply Mismatches

The variability of renewable energy often leads to mismatches between supply and demand. For example, solar power generation typically peaks during midday when electricity demand may be lower, while wind energy output is often highest at night. These mismatches can result in either surplus energy or energy shortages, creating inefficiencies in the system.

Challenges of Mismatches:

• **Economic Impact:** Excess energy generation can lead to lower electricity prices or wasted energy, reducing the economic viability of renewable energy projects.

• **Load Management:** Sudden surges or drops in energy supply require rapid adjustments to balance the grid, increasing operational complexity.

Demand-side management programs and energy storage systems offer potential solutions to align supply with demand more effectively.

Solutions to Intermittency Challenges

Addressing the challenges of intermittency requires a combination of technological advancements, policy support, and innovative system designs:

• **Energy Storage Systems:** Batteries, pumped hydro, and thermal storage can store excess energy during periods of high generation and release it when needed.

• **Grid Modernization:** Smart grids, advanced forecasting tools, and demand-response programs enable more flexible and adaptive energy systems.

• **Diversified Energy Mix:** Combining different renewable energy sources, such as solar, wind, and hydropower, reduces overall variability by leveraging complementary generation patterns.

• **Regional Integration:** Expanding interconnections between regions allows excess energy to be shared across borders, balancing supply and demand more effectively.

Policies for Energy Reliability in Renewable Energy Systems

As renewable energy becomes a significant component of global energy systems, ensuring energy reliability has become a critical priority for policymakers. Renewable energy sources, such as solar and wind, are inherently variable, posing challenges to maintaining a stable and continuous energy supply. Policies aimed at enhancing energy reliability play a vital role in addressing these challenges, supporting the seamless integration of renewables, and safeguarding grid stability.

The Importance of Energy Reliability

Energy reliability ensures that electricity is consistently available to meet demand, regardless of fluctuations in generation or consumption. A reliable energy system supports economic stability, public safety, and societal well-being. However, the variability of renewable energy sources introduces complexities in achieving this goal. For instance, solar panels produce electricity only during daylight hours, and wind turbines depend on wind conditions, leading to potential mismatches between supply and demand.

Policies that enhance reliability focus on mitigating these challenges through strategic planning, technology deployment, and market design. These measures are critical for ensuring that renewable energy systems can deliver dependable power while advancing sustainability goals.

Key Policy Instruments for Energy Reliability

1. **Energy Storage Incentives:**

Energy storage systems, such as batteries and pumped hydro storage, are essential for balancing supply and demand in renewable energy systems. Policies that incentivize the deployment of energy storage can enhance grid reliability by storing excess energy during periods of high generation and releasing it during periods of low generation.

• **Examples of Incentives:** Tax credits, grants, and subsidies for energy storage projects.

• **Impact:** Reduced reliance on fossil fuel-based backup power and improved grid flexibility.

2. **Grid Modernization Programs:**

Modernizing grid infrastructure is a key component of energy reliability policies. Upgrades to transmission and distribution networks enable grids to accommodate higher levels of renewable energy and improve their ability to handle variability.

• **Policy Measures:** Investments in smart grids, advanced metering infrastructure (AMI), and high-voltage transmission lines.

• **Benefits:** Enhanced grid resilience, reduced energy losses, and better integration of decentralized energy resources.

3. **Demand-Side Management (DSM):**

DSM policies encourage consumers to adjust their energy usage in response to grid conditions, reducing strain on the system during peak demand periods. These programs align electricity consumption with renewable energy availability, optimizing resource use.

• **Policy Tools:** Time-of-use pricing, demand-response programs, and incentives for energy-efficient appliances.

• **Outcome:** Improved load management and reduced need for costly peaking power plants.

4. Flexible Market Mechanisms:

Policies that promote flexibility in energy markets support reliability by enabling faster responses to changes in supply and demand. For example, capacity markets incentivize the availability of standby power resources, while ancillary services markets support grid stability through frequency and voltage regulation.

• **Policy Design:** Inclusion of renewables and energy storage in capacity and ancillary services markets.

• **Advantage:** Increased participation of renewable energy providers in ensuring grid reliability.

5. Renewable Energy Integration Standards:

Clear technical standards for connecting renewable energy systems to the grid are essential for ensuring reliability. Policies that mandate grid-friendly technologies, such as smart inverters and energy management systems, can reduce variability impacts.

• **Regulatory Measures:** Requirements for grid compatibility and support for renewable energy developers.

• **Effect:** Smoother integration of renewables and minimized disruptions to grid operations.

International and Regional Cooperation

In addition to national policies, international and regional collaboration is crucial for energy reliability. Cross-border electricity trade and interconnected grids allow countries to share renewable energy resources, balancing supply and demand across larger geographic areas.

• **Examples:** The European Union's Internal Energy Market and regional power pools in Africa and Asia.

• **Impact:** Enhanced energy security and reduced costs through shared infrastructure and resources.

Addressing Challenges in Policy Implementation

Despite their benefits, policies for energy reliability face several challenges:

1. **High Costs:** Implementing grid modernization and storage incentives requires significant investment. Governments must prioritize funding and explore public-private partnerships to share costs.

2. **Regulatory Barriers:** Outdated regulations may hinder the adoption of advanced technologies and market designs. Policymakers must establish clear frameworks that support innovation.

3. **Stakeholder Engagement:** Engaging utilities, consumers, and developers in policy design ensures that measures address diverse needs and encourage broad participation.

Future Directions

Policymakers must continue to evolve energy reliability measures to address emerging challenges and opportunities.

• **Incorporating Digital Solutions:** Leveraging AI, machine learning, and predictive analytics can enhance grid management and improve forecasting accuracy.

• **Fostering Innovation:** Supporting R&D in energy storage, smart grid technologies, and demand-response mechanisms will drive future improvements in reliability.

• **Promoting Equity:** Ensuring that energy reliability policies benefit all communities, including underserved and remote areas, is essential for achieving inclusive and sustainable energy systems.

Conclusion: Final Recommendations

The renewable energy transition is a global imperative, driven by the urgent need to address climate change, enhance energy security, and promote sustainable development. This book has explored the critical enablers and actions required to overcome the technical, financial, regulatory, and operational challenges associated with integrating renewable energy into modern energy systems. As we reach the conclusion, it is clear that a coordinated, multi-stakeholder approach is essential for achieving a reliable, equitable, and sustainable energy future.

This chapter synthesizes the key insights from previous chapters, offering actionable recommendations for policymakers, industry leaders, and other stakeholders. It emphasizes the importance of long-term planning, inclusive collaboration, and innovation in technology and policy. By focusing on these priorities, decision-makers can ensure that renewable energy not only becomes the cornerstone of the global energy system but also contributes to broader social and economic benefits. The chapter concludes with a call to action, underscoring the need for urgency and ambition in accelerating the renewable energy transition.

Summary of Key Enablers for Renewable Energy Transition

The global shift to renewable energy requires a comprehensive set of enablers to overcome challenges, scale deployment, and ensure the long-term sustainability of energy systems. These enablers span policy, regulation, technology, finance, infrastructure, and international collaboration, creating a foundation for achieving global energy and climate goals. This section provides a detailed summary of the key enablers discussed throughout this book, emphasizing their roles and interconnections in driving the renewable energy transition.

1. Policy and Regulation

Policies and regulatory frameworks are critical for creating an environment conducive to renewable energy adoption. They provide the legal and institutional foundation for renewable energy deployment while addressing market barriers and ensuring investor confidence.

Key Elements of Policy and Regulation:

• **Renewable Energy Targets:** Setting clear and ambitious national and regional targets creates a roadmap for renewable energy development. These targets signal commitment and attract investments.

• **Incentive Mechanisms:** Policies such as feed-in tariffs, tax credits, and renewable energy certificates incentivize developers and reduce the cost burden on consumers.

• **Streamlined Permitting Processes:** Simplifying and accelerating permitting for renewable energy projects ensures timely implementation and reduces administrative costs.

• **Grid Integration Standards:** Establishing technical standards for renewable energy interconnection promotes compatibility and minimizes disruptions to grid operations.

Effective policies and regulations must adapt to evolving technologies and market conditions, fostering innovation while ensuring reliability and affordability.

2. Financial Mechanisms

Financing renewable energy projects remains one of the most significant challenges for the energy transition. Innovative financial mechanisms play a critical role in reducing risks, mobilizing investments, and ensuring equitable access to resources.

Key Financial Enablers:

• **Blended Finance:** Combining public and private funding reduces risks for investors while leveraging public resources to attract additional capital.

• **Green Bonds and Climate Funds:** Instruments like green bonds and initiatives such as the GCF mobilize large-scale financing for renewable energy projects, particularly in developing countries.

• **Subsidies and Grants:** Targeted subsidies and grants help bridge financial gaps, making renewable energy systems more accessible to low-income communities.

• **Microfinance and Crowdfunding:** These mechanisms empower small-scale developers and communities to invest in decentralized renewable energy systems.

Financial enablers must address regional disparities, ensuring that underserved areas can access the resources needed for their energy transitions.

3. Technology and Innovation

Advancements in technology are central to overcoming the challenges of renewable energy integration, from variability and intermittency to storage and grid management. Continuous innovation ensures that renewable energy systems become more efficient, cost-effective, and adaptable.

Critical Technological Enablers:

• **Energy Storage:** Technologies like lithium-ion batteries, pumped hydro, and thermal storage address the variability of solar and wind energy, ensuring a reliable power supply.

• **Smart Grids:** Digital technologies, such as real-time monitoring, predictive analytics, and automation, enhance grid flexibility and optimize energy flows.

• **Advanced Forecasting:** Improved weather prediction models and AI-driven analytics enable better planning and management of renewable energy resources.

• **Decentralized Energy Solutions:** Microgrids, solar home systems, and community energy projects empower consumers while reducing reliance on centralized power systems.

Investing in R&D is crucial for fostering innovation and accelerating the deployment of these technologies.

4. Infrastructure Modernization

Modernizing energy infrastructure is essential for supporting the integration of renewable energy into existing systems. This includes upgrading transmission and distribution networks, enhancing grid resilience, and building new infrastructure to accommodate decentralized energy systems.

Key Infrastructure Requirements:

• **Expanded Transmission Networks:** High-voltage transmission lines enable the transport of renewable energy from remote generation sites to demand centers.

• **Energy Storage Integration:** Infrastructure for large-scale storage systems ensures that surplus energy is stored and dispatched as needed.

• **Decentralized Systems:** Investments in microgrids and off-grid solutions expand energy access in rural and remote areas.

• **Resilience Measures:** Climate-resilient infrastructure, such as underground cables and weather-resistant components, minimizes disruptions caused by extreme weather events.

Infrastructure investments must align with long-term planning to accommodate future growth in renewable energy capacity.

5. Workforce Development

A skilled workforce is a vital enabler of the renewable energy transition, ensuring that systems are designed, installed, operated, and maintained effectively. Workforce development programs address skill gaps and create employment opportunities across the energy value chain.

Strategies for Workforce Development:

• **Training and Certification Programs:** Providing specialized training ensures that workers have the skills needed for renewable energy technologies.

• **Educational Partnerships:** Collaborations between industry, academia, and governments promote the development of relevant curricula and research opportunities.

• **Gender and Diversity Initiatives:** Encouraging diversity in the renewable energy workforce ensures inclusivity and broadens the talent pool.

By prioritizing workforce development, stakeholders can create jobs, foster innovation, and strengthen the capacity for renewable energy deployment.

6. International Collaboration

Global challenges like climate change and energy access require coordinated international action. International collaboration facilitates knowledge sharing, technology transfer, and resource pooling, enabling countries to accelerate their renewable energy transitions.

Key Areas of Collaboration:

• **Multilateral Agreements:** Frameworks such as the Paris Agreement and the United Nations' SDGs provide a shared vision and commitments for renewable energy adoption.

• **Technology Transfer:** Collaborative initiatives ensure that developing countries have access to advanced renewable energy technologies and expertise.

• **Regional Energy Integration:** Cross-border energy trade and interconnected grids optimize renewable energy use and enhance energy security.

• **Capacity Building:** International organizations, such as the IRENA, provide technical assistance and training to support renewable energy initiatives.

Strengthening global partnerships ensures that the benefits of renewable energy are shared equitably, promoting sustainability and resilience.

Interconnections of All Strategies for Renewable Energy Transition

The renewable energy transition is not driven by isolated strategies but by the interconnectedness of various enablers, each complementing the other to create a cohesive and effective system. Policies, technology, finance, infrastructure, workforce development, and international collaboration are interdependent elements that collectively address the challenges of variability, scalability, and equity in renewable energy adoption. Understanding these interconnections is vital for stakeholders to design and implement integrated approaches that maximize the potential of renewable energy systems.

Policy as the Foundation

Policies serve as the foundation for all other strategies, setting the legal, regulatory, and institutional frameworks necessary for renewable energy deployment. Without supportive policies, advancements in technology or financing mechanisms may lack the structure needed to scale effectively.

Connections to Other Strategies:

• **Technology Development:** Policies that fund R&D drive innovation in renewable energy technologies, such as energy storage and smart grids.

• **Financing:** Incentive mechanisms like tax credits, subsidies, and renewable energy certificates attract investment and reduce project costs.

• **Infrastructure:** Regulatory standards ensure that grid modernization aligns with renewable energy integration goals.

• **Workforce Development:** Educational policies and training programs prepare the workforce for emerging needs in the renewable energy sector.

Policies act as the glue that binds all strategies, creating an environment where innovation and investment can thrive.

Technology and Infrastructure Integration

Technological innovation and infrastructure modernization are intrinsically linked, as new technologies often require upgraded infrastructure to operate effectively. For instance, smart grids rely on digital solutions to manage decentralized and variable renewable energy sources, while advanced storage technologies depend on resilient grid systems for optimal performance.

Examples of Interconnections:

• **Energy Storage and Grid Flexibility:** Storage systems stabilize grids by managing surplus energy during high renewable generation periods and supplying power during low output periods.

• **Decentralized Systems and Smart Grids:** Microgrids and DERs enhance energy access and efficiency when integrated with smart grid technologies.

• **Resilience and Technology:** Infrastructure investments in climate-resilient components, such as weather-resistant transmission lines, complement technological advancements in predictive analytics and automation.

Infrastructure and technology must evolve in tandem to support the growing share of renewables in energy systems.

Financing as the Catalyst

Finance is a critical enabler that intersects with every aspect of the renewable energy transition. Adequate funding is necessary to support R&D, deploy technologies, upgrade infrastructure, and implement training programs. Innovative financial mechanisms, such as blended finance and green bonds, also reduce risks and attract private sector investment.

Key Connections:

• **Policies and Incentives:** Financial incentives, backed by strong policy frameworks, make renewable energy projects economically viable.

• **Infrastructure Investments:** Large-scale projects, such as offshore wind farms or regional interconnections, rely on significant financing to cover upfront costs.

• **Technology Deployment:** Financing supports the commercialization of emerging technologies, bridging the gap between innovation and large-scale implementation.

• **Workforce Development:** Funding for educational initiatives ensures that the workforce can meet the technical demands of renewable energy systems.

Finance acts as the catalyst that transforms strategic plans into actionable projects, enabling progress across all domains.

Workforce Development and Economic Growth

The development of a skilled workforce intersects with policy, technology, and finance to ensure the successful implementation and management of renewable energy systems. A well-trained workforce not only supports deployment but also drives economic growth through job creation and local industry development.

Connections to Other Strategies:

• **Technology:** Training programs equip workers with the skills needed to operate, maintain, and innovate renewable energy technologies.

• **Policies:** Educational policies and government funding for vocational programs expand access to training opportunities.

• **Economic Impact:** Workforce development initiatives create jobs across the energy value chain, from manufacturing to maintenance, boosting local economies.

Workforce development ensures that human resources align with the technical and operational needs of renewable energy systems.

International Collaboration for Global Solutions

International collaboration ties together all strategies, promoting knowledge sharing, technology transfer, and equitable access to resources. Global partnerships address common challenges, such as climate change and energy access, by pooling expertise and resources.

Examples of Interconnections:

• **Technology and Knowledge Sharing:** Collaborative initiatives enable developing countries to access advanced technologies and expertise.

• **Financing Mechanisms:** Multilateral funds, such as the GCF, support renewable energy projects in underserved regions.

• **Infrastructure Development:** Regional energy interconnections allow countries to share renewable resources, balancing supply and demand across borders.

• **Policy Alignment:** International agreements, such as the Paris Agreement, create a unified framework for national renewable energy targets and initiatives.

Collaboration amplifies the impact of individual strategies, ensuring a more inclusive and sustainable energy transition.

Holistic Approach for Maximum Impact

The interconnectedness of these strategies highlights the need for a holistic approach to renewable energy transition. Addressing each enabler in isolation can lead to inefficiencies, delays, and missed opportunities for synergy. By designing integrated strategies, stakeholders can create systems that are not only effective but also resilient and adaptable to future challenges.

Recommendations for Policymakers

Policymakers play a central role in enabling the renewable energy transition by creating supportive frameworks, addressing barriers, and ensuring equitable access to resources. Strategic, forward-thinking policies can accelerate renewable energy adoption, drive innovation, and achieve long-term sustainability goals. The following recommendations outline key actions for policymakers to facilitate this transition.

1. Set Ambitious Renewable Energy Targets

Policymakers should establish clear and ambitious renewable energy targets aligned with global climate goals, such as the Paris Agreement. These targets provide direction for stakeholders, attract investments, and foster accountability. NDCs should integrate specific renewable energy goals, supported by actionable plans for implementation.

2. Provide Financial Incentives

Incentives such as feed-in tariffs, tax credits, and grants reduce the cost burden of renewable energy projects, encouraging investment and innovation. Policymakers should prioritize mechanisms that attract private sector financing while leveraging public funds to de-risk projects in underserved regions. Blended finance models can be particularly effective in mobilizing resources for large-scale and off-grid projects.

3. Support Grid Modernization

Investments in grid modernization are essential to accommodate the variability and decentralization of renewable energy. Policymakers should promote the adoption of smart grids, energy storage systems, and advanced metering infrastructure. Regulations must ensure that grid upgrades are aligned with renewable energy integration goals and address resilience to climate impacts.

4. Develop Workforce Training Programs

Policymakers should collaborate with industry and academia to design training programs that equip workers with the skills needed for renewable energy technologies. These programs should address technical, operational, and managerial competencies while ensuring inclusivity, particularly for underrepresented groups. Supporting workforce development ensures a steady supply of skilled professionals for the growing renewable energy sector.

5. Foster International Collaboration

Policymakers must strengthen international partnerships to share knowledge, technology, and financial resources. Participation in multilateral agreements and regional energy initiatives enables countries to align policies, leverage shared resources, and address common challenges. Collaborative platforms, such as the IRENA, provide valuable opportunities for coordination and capacity building.

6. Ensure Regulatory Certainty

Stable and transparent regulatory frameworks are critical for attracting investments in renewable energy. Policymakers should establish clear guidelines for project permitting, grid interconnection, and market participation. Regulations should also incentivize innovation, such as energy storage, and ensure fair access for distributed energy resources.

7. Address Energy Access and Equity

Policies must prioritize energy access for underserved and remote communities. Decentralized energy systems, supported by microgrids and off-grid solutions, can provide affordable and reliable electricity. Policymakers should ensure that benefits from renewable energy projects are equitably distributed, promoting social and economic inclusion.

Vision for a Renewable Energy Future

A renewable energy future envisions a world powered predominantly by clean, sustainable, and abundant energy sources such as solar, wind, hydropower, and geothermal. This future is characterized by energy systems that are reliable, resilient, and inclusive, addressing the global challenges of climate change, energy security, and equitable development.

In this vision, renewable energy becomes the cornerstone of economic growth and environmental stewardship. Decentralized energy systems empower communities, particularly in underserved and remote areas, by providing access to affordable and reliable electricity. Advanced technologies such as smart grids, energy storage, and artificial intelligence optimize energy generation, distribution, and consumption, ensuring efficiency and adaptability in an ever-evolving landscape.

A renewable energy future prioritizes equity and inclusivity, ensuring that the benefits of clean energy reach all, regardless of geography or socioeconomic status. International collaboration fosters the sharing of knowledge, technology, and resources, enabling global participation in the energy transition. Policies and investments align with sustainability goals, creating jobs, driving innovation, and reducing greenhouse gas emissions.

This future also emphasizes the interconnectedness of energy systems with other sectors, such as transportation, agriculture, and industry, promoting holistic approaches to sustainability. By accelerating the adoption of renewable energy, this vision offers not only a solution to energy challenges but also a pathway to a cleaner, healthier, and more prosperous planet for generations to come.

www.ingramcontent.com/pod-product-compliance
Lightning Source LLC
Chambersburg PA
CBHW052136270326
41930CB00012B/2908